BRITISH TAX LIBRARY

TAXATION OF COMPANIES

AND

COMPANY RECONSTRUCTIONS

First Supplement to the Sixth Edition

By

RICHARD BRAMWELL, Q.C., LL.M. (Lond.)
of the Middle Temple

MICHAEL HARDWICK, M.A. (Oxon.), LL.M. (Cantab.)
Solicitor, Partner in Linklaters & Paines

MARK KINGSTONE, M.A., B.C.L. (Oxon)
Solicitor, Partner in Linklaters & Paines

LONDON
SWEET & MAXWELL
1995

Published in 1995 by
Sweet & Maxwell Limited of
South Quay Plaza
183 Marsh Wall, London E14 9FT
Typeset by
Mendip Communications Ltd., Frome, Somerset
Printed in Great Britain by
Clay's Ltd., St Ives plc.

Main Work ISBN 0-421-52030-2
Supplement ISBN 0-421-54660-3

No natural forests were destroyed to make
this product. Farmed timber was used and replanted.

AUTHORS' NOTE

In the time since the publication of the main text, publication has commenced of the Inland Revenue's manuals. Whilst some material relevant to the contents of the main text has been released (for example, in the CGT manual), the corporation tax volume has yet to appear. In these circumstances we have decided to postpone any systematic study of the manuals until everything is to hand. Accordingly, there are no references to the manuals in this Supplement. Our impression, however, is that such references would not be copious because most technical points are concealed behind instructions to inspectors to consult the relevant specialist sections. There are though, words of comfort to be found of which the following is an example:

"... you should not challenge the transfer of assets from one group member to another at no gain/no loss under Section 171 TCGA 1992, where this brings gains and losses together in a single company, provided that both the gain and the loss are wholly attributable to changes in value while the assets were in the ownership of the group".

In due course we hope to be able to identify all such passages as may be of use to readers, but for the time being there is no alternative but to check the manuals themselves on a case by case basis.

RB
August 7, 1995

PUBLISHER'S NOTE

The first supplement to the sixth edition of *Taxation of Companies and Company Reconstructions* brings the work up to date to August 1, 1995. It takes into account all developments since the sixth edition was published in November 1994.

The supplement is paragraphed to correspond with the paragraphs as they appear in the main work. For example, paragraph 6–22 of the supplement will amend paragraph 6–22 of the main work. This enables the reader to refer quickly and easily between the main work and the supplement.

CONTENTS

TABLE OF CASES

(References are to Paragraph numbers)

TABLE OF STATUTES

TABLE OF STATUTORY INSTRUMENTS

(References are to Paragraph numbers)

PART I
TAXATION OF COMPANIES
IN GENERAL

CHAPTER 2

THE CHARGE TO CORPORATION TAX AND COMPUTATION OF PROFITS

I. THE CHARGE TO CORPORATION TAX

Schedule A income

The revision of Schedule A made by the Finance Act 1995 applies for the **2–04A** purposes of income tax only: section 37(1). Accordingly, the new scheme is relevant only to non-resident companies with Schedule A sources: see paragraph 15–27 of this Supplement.

II. SPECIAL TYPES OF COMPANIES

Companies carrying on a mutual business

The Special Commissioners have held that the mutuality principle applies to **2–34** transactions between a club and non-voting associate members.[1]

[1] *Westbourne Supporters of Glentoran Club v. Brennan SC* 00022 (1995).

CHAPTER 3

CHARGES ON INCOME, WITHHOLDING TAX AND CHARITABLE DONATIONS

II. CHARGES ON INCOME

Replace footnote 3 on p. 38 of the main work with the following: The Inland **3–02**

Revenue regard interest on advances as "payable in the United Kingdom" even if it was not so paid provided that the loan agreement permits payment to be made both within and outside the United Kingdom and the interest falls to be brought into account as a trading receipt of the bank's bona fide banking business in the United Kingdom (and it is so brought into account). The same applies, but only to foreign currency loans, where the loan agreement requires payment to be made outside the United Kingdom. For a more detailed discussion of this point see paragraph 3–24A of this Supplement.

3–04   In the third line of the second paragraph on p. 40 of the main work, "discharge" should read "discharged".

V. Withholding Tax

3–24A   On January 30, 1995, the Inland Revenue revised their practice regarding the circumstances in which they will regard interest as "payable in the United Kingdom".[1] See paragraph 3–24 of the main work for the previous position. The Inland Revenue's revised practice is that interest will be treated as payable in the United Kingdom for the purposes of section 349(3)(a) of the Taxes Act 1988 and consequently as not liable to deduction of income tax at source provided that the interest is payable on an advance and falls to be, and accordingly is, brought into account as a trading receipt of the business carried on by the bank in the United Kingdom, even if the loan agreement permits payment to be made both within and outside the United Kingdom. The practice also applies to Sections 337(3) and 338(3)(b) of the Taxes Act 1988.

This revised practice is wider than the existing practice in two respects. It extends the practice to sterling loans and to Section 338(3)(b) of the Taxes Act 1988. The revised practice is effective from January 30, 1995 but the Inland Revenue have made it clear that where a taxpayer has taken advantage of the existing practice, that practice will continue to apply to existing transactions, where that is to the taxpayer's benefit.

The revised practice is more restrictive than the original in that it does not extend to situations in which the loan agreement specifically requires the payment of interest to be made not in the United Kingdom but abroad. This caused some potential difficulties as foreign currency loan agreements will often specify that payment should only be made outside the United Kingdom, typically in the relevant foreign jurisdiction. As a result of representations on this point, the Inland Revenue published an Extra Statutory Concession on February 22, 1995[2] making it clear that the revised practice would also effectively apply to a foreign currency advance even where the loan agreement required payment to be made outside the United Kingdom. The Extra Statutory Concession applies to any loan agreement entered into on or after January 30, 1995, the date on which the revised practice came into effect.

3–25   Replace footnote 7 with the following: Within the meaning of *ibid*. s.841. The Inland Revenue published a list of stock exchanges designated as "recognised stock exchanges" in Inland Revenue Tax Bulletin, December 1994 at p. 186.

[1] See SP1/95: 1995 S.T.I. 182 and 184.
[2] ESC C26: 1995 S.T.I. 346.

CHAPTER 4

COMPLIANCE

Contents   *Para.*
  I. Introduction   4–01
    Assessment of persons other
      than the company   4–06

I. INTRODUCTION

Assessment of persons other than the company

The Revenue has published its practice in applying section 767A: see [1994] **4–06**
S.T.I. 1291.

CHAPTER 5 ·

CAPITAL ALLOWANCES FOR MACHINERY AND PLANT

Contents	*Para.*	Contents	*Para.*
I. Meaning of Plant	5–01	**II. The Scheme of the Allowances**	5–10
"Plant"	5–02	The allowances and charges	5–10

I. MEANING OF PLANT

"Plant"·

The Revenue has stated that for the purposes of the CGT exemption for **5–02**
"machinery", the normal meaning of the word applies, namely, "any apparatus
which applies mechanical power". In particular, this covers antique clocks.[1] On
the same basis, such items qualify for capital allowances if bought for business
purposes.

[1] [1994] STI 1290.

II. THE SCHEME OF THE ALLOWANCES

The allowances and charges

5–10   Where, on or after April 6, 1995 a company with an existing trade commences a separate trade part way through an accounting period, allowances for that accounting period in respect of the new trade are reduced in proportion to the part of the accounting period then expired: CAA 1992 s.24(2)(a)(ii) as inserted by F.A. 1994 s.213(4) and s.218(1A).

CHAPTER 6

FIXTURES

Contents   *Para.*

I. FIXTURES AS PLANT

6–13   Note 18: affirmed [1995] S.T.C. 706.

II. OWNERSHIP OF FIXTURES

Equipment lessors: sections 53 and 58

6–23   The Revenue has confirmed that section 53 applies irrespective of whether an asset becomes a fixture before it is leased.[1] A further point of practice is that elections are allowed only after the commencement of the lessee's trade.[2]

It is understood that *Melluish v. BMI* is to be heard by the House of Lords. A point not discussed in either of the two judgments to date is how, on the facts, the requirements of section 53(1)(b) were met:

> . "(b) an agreement is entered into for the lease, directly or indirectly from the equipment lessor, of the machinery or plant (otherwise than as part of the relevant land) to another person ("the equipment lessee") *for the purposes of a trade carried on by the equipment lessee or for leasing otherwise than in the course of a trade*".

In so far as the equipment was installed in council houses then it fell within the closing words (leasing by the equipment lessee otherwise than in the course of trade). The equipment installed in swimming baths and crematoria was used by the local authority in carrying on a trade (albeit one outside the charge to tax). However, the equipment installed in the municipal offices[3] does not appear to have fallen under either head.

[1] [1994] STI 1288.
[2] *Ibid.*
[3] See [1994] S.T.C. at p. 338.

CHAPTER 7

LOSSES

I. TRADING LOSSES

Carry forward against future trading income

In *Nuclear Electric plc v. Bradley*,[1] the question arose of whether income from a   **7–03** fund to meet future trade liabilities was within the relief for carried forward losses. The liabilities were discounted and the fund was invested so as to produce a rate of return equal to the discount. The Special Commissioners held that as the fund was not in any way dedicated to the future liabilities, and as the liabilities might be met without recourse to the fund, the income was not within the relief. In the High Court, that decision was reversed because of the correlation between the rate of discount and the rate of return. It is likely that this case will go further.

Case V losses and uncommercial trades

For an illuminating decision on the application of the uncommercial trades   **7–06.** legislation to a business "blown off course" by an economic recession, see *Walls v. Livesey*, a decision of the Special Commissioners.[2]

[1] [1995] STC 285.
[2] SC 000004 (1995).

CHAPTER 10

THE RAMSAY DOCTRINE

Contents   *Para.*

I. THE RAMSAY PRINCIPLE

Exploring the limits of *Furniss v. Dawson*

10–09A   In *Pigott v. Staines Investments*[1] a series of events separated by ten months were held to have been "preordained", yet it was further held that the transaction in question could not be recharacterised so as to remove the tax advantage to the participants. The case is important and requires a full exposition.

The tax advantage arose out of the acquisition of a company with capacity to carry back ACT. The acquiring group (BAT) had been paying dividends out of foreign earnings that had not borne corporation tax in full. Before the change in the law made by F.A. 1993, it was possible to mitigate that disadvantage by using the carry back capacity of a company that had earned corporation tax profits in another group (see paragraph 12–25). BAT acquired from Tesco a company (Staines) that had been the main operating company of the Tesco group but which by the time of the acquisition had become a shell company. The idea was that Staines would become an intermediate holding company in the BAT group, and as such would receive group income (out of post-acquisition profits) from an operating company. That income would be redistributed outside the group election, the corresponding ACT being carried back to earlier accounting periods in which Staines had paid corporation tax. Staines had the capacity to carry back about £58m. of ACT.

Staines was purchased in February 1991 under an agreement by which BAT paid an amount equal to the net assets of Staines and further agreed to pay to Tesco an amount equal to half the ACT carried back up to a maximum of £27.5m. BAT agreed to take certain steps towards achieving the carry back, and these included transferring to Staines an operating subsidiary whose post-acquisition profits for its current accounting period were likely to be such as to enable it to pay a dividend of £165m. BAT further agreed to use its best endeavours to procure Staines to pay a non-group dividend of up to £165m., but the whole agreement was subject to a proviso that BAT was not obliged to procure the payment of any dividends it considered to be imprudent. Accordingly, BAT had no obligation to Tesco except to the extent that the operating subsidiary (BAT Co) had post acquisition profits in the current or succeeding accounting period. Even then, any obligation would have been extinguished by the enactment of legislation preventing the carry back by Staines of ACT (as happened in 1993).

The events that happened were as follows: immediately after the acquisition of Staines in February 1991, BAT Co became a subsidiary of Staines. Ten months later, in December 1991, BAT Co paid a group dividend to Staines of £176.6m., and on the next day Staines paid a non-group dividend of the same amount to BAT. Staines claimed to carry back the ACT of £58.6m.

The Inspector refused the claim on the basis that:

(a) the transactions described above were a preordained series; and
(b) the payment of the non-group dividend fell to be treated as a contractual payment and not as a distribution.

This would have given Staines no ACT liability, but equally, BAT would have had no franked investment income out of which to pay dividends to shareholders.

The Special Commissioner held that the transactions were preordained, but that they could not be recharacterised so as to give effect to the Inspector's contention. In the High Court both aspects of the Special Commissioner's decision were upheld.

On the preordination point, Staines accepted that the second dividend was preordained at the time of the first, but this was not sufficient for the purposes of the Crown's argument because the claimed recharacterisation depended on a notional contract between BAT, BAT Co, Staines and Tesco. Under this supposed contract, Staines had an obligation to hand on to BAT the dividend from BAT Co, the point of the argument being to deprive the group dividend received by Staines the character of distributable profits in the hands of Staines.[2] No argument was advanced that the existence of Staines could be disregarded so as to treat the group dividend as going direct to BAT: the Crown specifically accepted that the enduring existence of Staines had to be recognised, and the contractual argument sought to side-step this difficulty.

In the High Court the contractual argument was rejected as being an impossible analysis of a "perfectly ordinary transaction".[3] The Court went so far as to say that even if in reality there had been a contract of the kind contended for, this would not have altered the legal analysis of the distributions. However, the Court did uphold the Special Commissioner's decision that there was here a preordained series of transactions, and it is to this aspect of the decision that we now turn.

The preordination issue was approached on the basis that events are preordained if there is no practical likelihood that the later events will not follow the earlier ones. For Staines it was argued that this test was not satisfied having regard to a number of possibilities, for example, that BAT Co might not have earned substantial post-acquisition profits or that there might have been a change in the law to prevent the carry back. It was also argued that the ten month interval was in any event sufficient to negative preordination. The Court held that an extended interval cannot of itself negative preordination, and that the assessment of the probabilities here was within the limits of judgment allowed to the Commissioner. The authors do find it easy to accept that preordination is simply a matter of assessing probabilities. The nature of the series of events has to that of a "single and indivisible process" (see paragraph 10–09), and this concept cannot be applied to a transaction that requires commercial profits to be earned over a ten month period.

10–09B   A second decision that helps to mark out the limits of *Furniss* is *IRC v. McGuckian*.[4] In that case the following events fell to be considered:

(i)   trustee shareholders in B Co assigned their right to a dividend in return for a lump sum equal to 99 per cent of the dividend;

(ii)   a dividend was declared;

(iii)   the dividend was paid to the assignee;

(iv)   their assignee paid the purchase price to the trustees.

These events were preordained and had tax avoidance as their sole reason, but the Court declined to disregard the assignment. The main reason was that it was the whole substance of the transaction and so could not be called an inserted step. This may perhaps be an over strict view. Another consideration was that there was a specific anti-avoidance provision covering the sale of the right to dividends, but the authors do not see the relevance of this, unless there is a possibility of double taxation.

[1] [1995] STC 114.
[2] *Ibid*. at p. 141d–e.
[3] *Ibid*. at p. 142.
[4] [1994] STC 888.

CHAPTER 11

DISTRIBUTIONS AND STOCK DIVIDEND OPTIONS

III. DISTRIBUTIONS IN RESPECT OF SECURITIES

Interest payable to a non-resident associated company: section 209(2)(da)

11–36   In paragraph 17–20 of the main work it was pointed out that the rules treating payments of interest to non-resident associates as distributions might be invalid under E.U. law. The force of this point was recognised in the Press Release to the 1994 Budget[1] where it was explained that the thin capitalisation legislation was being amended to take account of the requirements of E.U. law. Whether the new rules attain their object is discussed in paragraph 17–20A of this Supplement. In this paragraph it is assumed they take effect according to their terms.

From November 29, 1994[2] (or April 1, 1995 in the case of interest paid gross under the Regulations discussed in paragraph 3–26 of the main work[3]), sections 209(2)(e)(iv) and (v) are repealed so that the rules set out in paragraph 11–36 of the main work cease to apply. From that date section 209(2)(da) comes into force, the main effect of which is that where interest is paid to a non-resident associate, only so much of the interest as is referable to the special relationship is treated as a distribution.

The effect of these changes is four-fold. For companies paying interest to non-resident associates who are entitled to the benefit of a double taxation agreement whose interest article overrode domestic United Kingdom law subject to a special relationship provision there should be no substantive change. The wording of the interest article of the United Kingdom/Spain double taxation agreement appears to prevent the application of the new[4] provisions, subject to a requirement that the amount of the interest paid in respect of the debt does not exceed that which would have been paid in the absence of any special relationship.[5]

In the case of interest paid to non-resident associates who are not entitled to the benefit of a double taxation agreement (perhaps because they are located in a tax haven jurisdiction) the position has improved immeasurably—whereas before any interest was treated as a distribution,[6] now interest can be paid without danger of recharacterisation to the extent that it would also have been paid, had the companies been unconnected.[7] The same applies in any case where the interest article of an appropriate double taxation agreement did not override domestic United Kingdom law.

The greatest adverse impact arises where previously the interest article of a double taxation agreement overrode domestic United Kingdom law but was not subject to a special relationship provision[8]—there will now be a limit on deductibility whereas previously there was not.

The existence of a direction given by the Inland Revenue pursuant to which interest is paid gross to a non-resident (see above) will not automatically mean that the new provisions will not apply in respect of such an interest payment, even where there is no change in circumstances. Such a direction cannot override domestic legislation. It may, however, mean that the Inland Revenue do not seek to apply the new provisions.

Although debt:equity ratios will be relevant, they will not be determinative— everything will depend on the facts of the particular case. However, in practice it is likely that where a company has a debt:equity ratio of no more than 1:1[9] and where its income cover is at least 3:1, a thin capitalisation argument is unlikely to be taken.

It is understood that in practice the Inland Revenue seek to be flexible— perhaps allowing, in problematic cases, the injection of additional equity capital or permitting part of the debt to be interest free, provided interest bearing debt is repaid in preference to interest free debt.

An article in the Tax Bulletin[10] outlines the Inland Revenue's approach to the new provisions and indicates how guidance may be obtained.

The structure of the legislation is to be noted. Section 209(2)(e)(iv)(v) specifically referred to payments to non-residents. The new sub-paragraph (2)(da) is not so restricted. However, it is subject to section 212 which provides that any interest paid out of the assets of a company to another company "which is within the charge to corporation tax" is not a distribution where the other conditions of the section are met. The application of section 212 is considered more fully in paragraph 11–36B below.

The special relationship

11–36A   The new section 209(2)(da) provides that "distribution" includes:

"(da) any interest or other distribution out of assets of the company ('the issuing company') in respect of securities issued by that company which are held by another company where—

(i) the issuing company is a 75 per cent subsidiary of the other company or both are 75 per cent subsidiaries of a third company, and

(ii) the whole or any part of the distribution represents an amount which would not have fallen to be paid to the other company if the companies had been companies between whom there was (apart from in respect of the securities in question) no relationship, arrangements or other connection (whether formal or informal),

except so much, if any, of any such distribution as does not represent such an amount or as is a distribution by virtue of paragraph (d) above or an amount representing the principal secured by the securities;"

The sub-section applies where the company issuing the securities[11] (the "issuing company") and the company holding the securities (the "associated company") are associated, namely, the issuing company is a 75 per cent subsidiary of the other or both are 75 per cent subsidiaries of a third company.[12] There is no requirement that the security is issued to the associated company, so an assignment by a third party to the associated company would be caught.

The effect of the sub-section is to turn interest or any other distribution out of the assets of the issuing company (for example, discounts)[13] into a distribution[14] *to the extent that* it only falls to be paid as a result of a relationship, arrangements or some other connection (whether formal or informal)[15] between the issuing company and the associated company. Any interest in excess of an arm's length amount will be treated as a distribution.

As such, the principle is simply stated and, arguably, the draftsman need have gone no further. Unfortunately, an attempt is made to set out in detail what factors are, or are not, to be taken into account. This results in 1½ pages of impenetrable[16] legislation[17] which fails to work in any readily intelligible way.

The legislation is less than user friendly. Rather than set out a list of relevant/irrelevant factors the draftsman seeks to incorporate by reference the factors relevant to the interpretation of the "special relationship" provision of a double taxation convention (see paragraph 15–34 of the main work).[18]

In considering whether, as a result of any relationship, arrangements or other connection[19] between the issuing company and the associated company, the amount of interest exceeds that which would otherwise have been paid, account must be taken of *all* factors including:

12

1. whether the loan would have been made at all;
2. the amount which the loan would have been; and
3. the rate of interest and other terms which would have been agreed

in each case, in the absence of the relationship.[20]

The Inland Revenue have indicated[21] that the most important factors are likely to be: the business sector of the company concerned (for example, is it a property owning company or a service company); the nature of, and title to, any assets which might provide security; cash flow; and the general state of the economy.

The Inland Revenue take the view that the legislation applies where, even though a loan could have been obtained from a third party on the same terms, the transaction would not have taken place but for the group relationship. The example given by the Inland Revenue in this context[22] is instructive, albeit somewhat unrealistic. A company has a fixed-term third-party loan bearing interest at LIBOR plus 1 per cent which still has three years to run at the relevant time. This loan is repaid and replaced by a three year intra-group loan carrying interest at LIBOR plus 1.5 per cent but which otherwise has terms and conditions identical to the third-party loan it replaces. Interest rates having increased since the original loan was obtained, LIBOR plus 1.5 per cent is an arm's length rate for a three year loan at the time the new loan is made. The Inland Revenue's view is that, as there is no commercial rationale for re-financing the existing loan at a higher rate of interest, the interest on the new loan only falls to be paid because of the group relationship and therefore all the interest constitutes a distribution. This is, perhaps, somewhat surprising in that it might only have been expected that the additional 0.5 per cent interest would be so characterised.

The article in the Tax Bulletin seems rather confused in that the Inland Revenue begin by saying they do not favour "crude" debt:equity ratios but then go on to indicate that they have in recent years tended to accept a debt:equity ratio of 1:1 and income cover of 3:1 as indicating that there are no thin capitalisation concerns.

One therefore has to consider carefully how the relationship between the issuing company and the associated company affects the amount of interest payable.

By allowing all factors to be taken into account, the above test would permit, in the following scenario, account to be taken of the guarantee by the non-resident parent in determining the amount of interest payable:

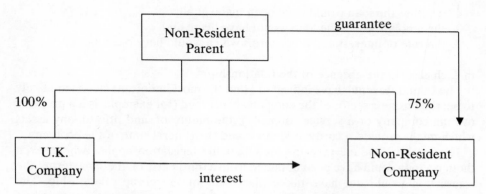

The existence of the guarantee by the non-resident parent of the obligations of the United Kingdom resident company may, therefore, permit a higher level of borrowing than would otherwise have been the case. Perhaps, without such a guarantee, the United Kingdom resident would not have been able to borrow at all, either from the non-resident or from a third party.

The Inland Revenue, however, wish to make clear the factors that can be taken into account and so in determining:

1. the appropriate level or extent of the issuing company's overall indebtedness;
2. whether it might be expected that the issuing company and the particular person would have become parties to a transaction involving the issue of a security by the issuing company or the making of a loan, or a loan of a particular amount, to the issuing company; and
3. the rate of interest and other terms that might be expected to be applicable in any particular case to such a transaction[23]

no account is to be taken of (or of any inference capable of being drawn from) any other[24] relationship (whether formal or informal) between the issuing company and any person *except* where that person is either:

1. not connected with the issuing company; or
2. is a company that is a member of the same U.K. grouping as the issuing company.[25]

In the above example, the guarantee would therefore be ignored in determining how much interest would be payable in arm's length circumstances by the issuing company because the non-resident parent is "connected" (see below) with the issuing company and is not a member of the same "U.K. grouping" (see below) as the issuing company.

The guarantee could be taken into account, so justifying the level of debt incurred by the issuing company, if it were from an unconnected third party or were given by a United Kingdom resident subsidiary of the issuing company, a member of a U.K. grouping, perhaps one owning a valuable asset.

A person is "connected" with the issuing company if he is connected within the terms of section 839 of the Taxes Act 1988 or if he (without being so connected) is:

(i) an effective 51 per cent subsidiary[26] of the issuing company; or

(ii) a company of which the issuing company is an effective 51 per cent subsidiary.[27]

The definition of a "U.K. grouping" is more complex.[28]

The members of a U.K. grouping are to be determined as follows:

1. where the issuing company has no effective 51 per cent subsidiaries and is not an effective 51 per cent subsidiary of a company resident in the United Kingdom—the issuing company[29]

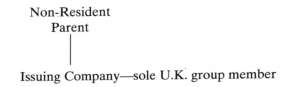

Non-Resident
Parent

Issuing Company—sole U.K. group member

2. where the issuing company has one or more effective 51 per cent subsidiaries and is not an effective 51 per cent subsidiary of a company resident in the United Kingdom—the issuing company and its effective 51 per cent subsidiaries[30]

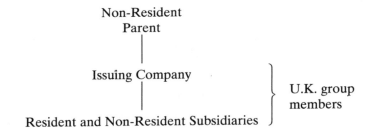

Non-Resident
Parent

Issuing Company

Resident and Non-Resident Subsidiaries

U.K. group members

3. where the issuing company is an effective 51 per cent subsidiary of a company resident in the United Kingdom (a "U.K. holding company")—any U.K. holding company which is not an effective 51 per cent subsidiary of any other U.K. holding company, and all its effective 51 per cent subsidiaries[31]

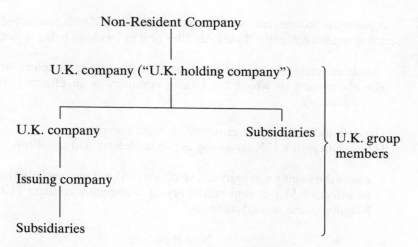

Whether or not one company is an effective 51 per cent subsidiary of another is to be determined in accordance with the provisions of Section 170(7) of the Taxation of Chargeable Gains Act 1992 (see paragraph 23–04 of the main work).[32]

When making such a determination, the question whether the effective 51 per cent subsidiaries of a resident company (the "putative holding company") include either the issuing company or a company of which the issuing company is an effective 51 per cent subsidiary shall be answered without regard to any beneficial entitlement[33] or the putative holding company to any profits or assets of any company resident outside the United Kingdom. Tracing through non-residents is therefore not permitted.

This is perhaps best illustrated by two examples:

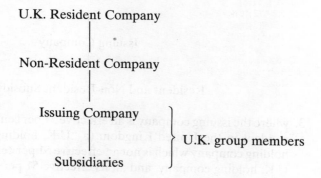

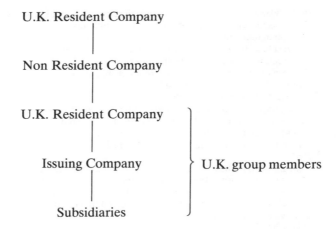

U.K. Resident Company

|

Non Resident Company

|

U.K. Resident Company ⎫

| ⎬ U.K. group members

Issuing Company ⎬

| ⎭

Subsidiaries

Exception for interest paid to certain resident companies

As mentioned, section 209(2)(da) is subject to the exceptions in section 212. The **11–36B** main effect of section 212 is to except payments of interest to resident companies that do not enjoy any blanket exemptions from tax[34] or any specific exemption in respect of interest.[35] There is a further exception for interest paid to charities or the bodies mentioned in section 507.[36]

---

[1] [1994] S.T.I. 1495.

[2] F.A. 1995 s.87(7).

[3] *Ibid.* s.87(8) (where the notice was given before November 29).

[4] (S.I. 1976 No. 1919), Art. 11(6).

[5] *Ibid.* Art. 11(8).

[6] *Ibid.* s.209(2)(e)(iv)(v).

[7] *Ibid.* s.209(2)(da).

[8] As is the case in the United Kingdom's double taxation treaties with Austria, Barbados, The Faroe Islands, Fiji, Germany, Israel, Japan, Kenya, Luxembourg, South Africa, the Sudan and Zambia.

[9] In Germany, in the case of holding companies, the ratio can be up to 9:1.

[10] Inland Revenue Tax Bulletin, June 1995, p. 218.

[11] As defined in I.C.T.A. 1988, s.254(1)—see para. 11–32 of the main work.

[12] *Ibid.* s.209(2)(da)(i).

[13] For ease of reference, subsequently referred to simply as "interest".

[14] Except to the extent either (i) already treated as a distribution by virtue of *ibid.* s.209(2)(d) (which treats interest or any other distribution out of assets in respect of securities as a distribution to the extent that such interest or other distribution exceeds a reasonable commercial return for the principal secured) or (ii) that the distribution represents the principal secured by the securities: *ibid.* s.209(2)(da). There is obviously scope for overlap between *ibid.* s.209(2)(d) and s.209(2)(da).

[15] Not including the securities in question.

[16] An overworked, but entirely apt, description of much recent legislation. In the Standing Committee debate, the Financial Secretary was forced to confess that these provisions would "not win clause of the year award for clarity of purpose and tidiness of construction": H.C. Official Reports, Standing Committee D (Thirteenth Sitting), col. 398. There was also a reference to "unintelligible gobbledegook": *ibid.* col. 403. The Financial Secretary indicated that the Inland Revenue would continue to provide guidance to taxpayers based on the precise facts of the case and intentions of the parties. In addition, the Inland Revenue would, in a Tax Bulletin article, explain its understanding of how the new provisions will operate: *ibid.* col. 401. See Inland Revenue Tax Bulletin, June 1995, p. 218.

[17] *Ibid.* s.209(8A) to (8F).

[18] *Ibid*. s.808A(2) to (4), in respect of which reference should be made to para. 15–34 of the main text. The "special relationship" provision of a double taxation agreement is relevant where the double taxation agreement reduces the withholding tax on interest payments and where interest paid to a non-resident is recharacterised as a distribution—in the latter case, it operates to limit the recharacterisation to the excessive interest.

[19] For ease of reference, the phrase "relationship, arrangements or other connection" is subsequently simply referred to as "relationship".

[20] *Ibid*. s.209(8A)(a). Presumably, where a security is issued to the associated company, all factors will be investigated as at the date of issue. When a security is assigned to the associated company, it is not clear whether the relevant date is the date of issue or date of assignment. In a Tax Bulletin article, the Inland Revenue refer to the date of assignment: Tax Bulletin, June 1995, p. 219.

[21] Inland Revenue Tax Bulletin, June 1995 p. 219.

[22] *Ibid*.

[23] *Ibid*. s.209(8B). These factors are similar, but not identical, to those listed in *ibid*. s.808A(2).

[24] The use of the word "other" is odd—it appears to contrast the relationship under consideration with that between the issuing company and the associated company in *ibid*. s.209(8B)(a). It would have been clearer if *ibid*. s.209(8B)(b) had referred to a relationship "between the issuing company and any *other* person" (emphasis added).

[25] *Ibid*. s.209(8A)(b). Whereas a third party lender would look at the borrower's group as a whole and might well accept and rely upon the guarantee of a non-resident parent, the legislation requires relationships with other group companies (such as non-resident parents) generally to be ignored, only being taken into account where the company concerned is part of a U.K. grouping.

[26] Determined in accordance with T.C.G.A. 1992, s.170(7): I.C.T.A. 1988, s.209(8E). References in *ibid*. s.209(8E) to a non-resident company do not include references to a company which is a dual resident company for the purposes of *ibid*. s.404 (see para. 15–51 of the main work).

[27] *Ibid*. s.209(8C).

[28] *Ibid*. s.209(8D). References in *ibid*. s.209(8D) to a non-resident company do not include references to a company which is a dual resident company for the purposes of *ibid*. s.404.

[29] *Ibid*. s.209(8D)(a).

[30] *Ibid*. s.209(8D)(b).

[31] *Ibid*. s.209(8D)(c).

[32] *Ibid*. s.209(8E).

[33] This appears to cover only a direct, not an indirect, beneficial entitlement.

[34] Such companies are "within the charge to corporation tax" (*ibid*. s.212(1)(a)) as that expression is defined by *ibid*. s.832(1). An example of a company enjoying a blanket exemption is a local authority association: *ibid*. s.519(2). A non-resident company trading in the U.K. through a branch or agency is "within the charge to corporation tax", but is cut out of the exception, other than in respect of interest attributable to the U.K. branch or agency, by the closing words of *ibid*. s.212(3).

[35] s.212(3) (the opening words). An example of a company enjoying an exemption for interest is the Atomic Energy Authority: *ibid*. s.512(1)(b).

[36] *Ibid*. s.212(4).

CHAPTER 12

ADVANCE CORPORATION TAX AND FRANKED INVESTMENT INCOME

I. ADVANCE CORPORATION TAX

Surrender of ACT to a subsidiary

The Inland Revenue have published in the Tax Bulletin[1] their practice in relation to claims to surrender ACT. Such claims need not specify the precise amount to be surrendered. Formula claims are acceptable. The Revenue consider that claim to surrender ACT cannot take advantage of an event occurring after the date of the claim but can take account of any claim which could have been made at the date of the claim to surrender ACT. A company can withdraw a claim to surrender ACT before it has been determined. If, therefore, an event occurs after a claim has been made which increases the amount of ACT which could be surrendered the company can withdraw the original claim and make a new claim, provided that the time limit for doing so has not expired.

12–18

The Inland Revenue consider that until a claim has been determined the subsidiary to which ACT has been surrendered cannot properly take the benefit of the surrendered ACT. This is a surprising conclusion because section 240(1) I.C.T.A. 1988 provides that a company may surrender ACT "on *making* a claim" and section 240(2) then provides that the surrendered ACT "shall be treated for the purposes of section 239" as having been paid by the company to which the ACT was surrendered. There is nothing about the Revenue having to determine the claim and, indeed, if the Revenue are correct they could frustrate a claim simply by failing to determine it. In any event, the point is largely academic because the Revenue go on to say that where a valid claim has been made and the surrendered ACT is entered in the subsidiary's tax return, they will generally not seek to collect corporation tax if the amount unpaid does not exceed the amount of the expected benefit.

II. FRANKED INVESTMENT INCOME

Set-off of losses, etc., against surplus franked investment income

12–31   With effect from an appointed day, it will be necessary for a claim to set losses off against franked investment income to be made in a return or an amended return.[2]

Franked investment income is defined as:

> "income of *a company resident in the United Kingdom* which consists of a distribution in respect of which the company is entitled to a tax credit..."

It follows that under domestic legislation only a United Kingdom resident company can set losses off against surplus franked investment income. The question sometimes arises whether the non discrimination article in a double tax treaty may permit a non resident company to seek similar relief. For example, the Double Tax Treaty between the United Kingdom and Switzerland provides:

> "The taxation on a permanent establishment which an enterprise of [Switzerland] has in the [United Kingdom] shall not be less favourably levied in [the United Kingdom] than the taxation levied on enterprises of [the United Kingdom] carrying on the same activities."[3]

Could a Swiss company with a United Kingdom branch successfully argue that it was less favourably taxed than a United Kingdom company because it could not claim to set branch losses off against dividend income and recover the tax credit? The Inland Revenue consider that the non discrimination article does not go this far.[4]

The point is a finely balanced one. If one focusses simply on the right to set losses off against dividend income and reclaim the tax credit, it looks as though the Swiss company's claim ought to succeed. A United Kingdom resident company can make such a claim but the Swiss company cannot. Therefore it is taxed less favourably.

On the other hand, if one looks at the provisions on franked investment income in context the position becomes less clearcut. These provisions ensure that a profitable United Kingdom company can redistribute dividend income without having to pay ACT while a loss making company can use its losses to reclaim the tax credit. While a Swiss company cannot use branch losses to reclaim a tax credit it is also not subject to ACT when it redistributes its income. It is less clear that in overall terms it is taxed less favourably.

The question also arises whether E.U. law might permit a claim by an E.U. resident company with a United Kingdom branch to set off branch losses against United Kingdom dividend income. It is thought that such a claim based on Article 52 of the E.C. Treaty might well fail either on the basis that an E.U. company is not in a comparable situation to a United Kingdom resident company in this regard[5] or on the basis of the coherence of the United Kingdom tax system,[6] although the contrary is certainly arguable.

Purchase of Own Shares as an Abnormal Dividend

In *USSL v. IRC*,[7] the application of Circumstance A of section 704 fell to be **12–42A** considered in relation to a Sched. F purchase of own shares from an exempt approved pension scheme. Although a purchase of own shares is not a dividend in the company law sense, any "qualifying distribution" is a dividend for the purposes of section 704.[8] As mentioned in paragraph 12–43 of the main text, it has been held that an exempt body does not obtain a tax advantage by securing a payment of the tax credit by virtue of its exemption. Accordingly, the Special Commissioner had to allow the appeal on this ground, the purpose of the proceedings being to challenge on appeal the correctness of *Sheppard v. IRC*.[9] However, the decision reviewed other points in the case. In particular, in relation to the question of whether the dividend was "abnormal", the Commissioner held that the speculative nature of the investment was material (*cf.* paragraph 12–42 of the main text) and that the Revenue had not discharged the onus of showing that on the facts, the return was abnormal. Another complication here was that the consideration for the shares included "moneys worth" in the form of an agreement to accept a low rate of return on a loan, and the value of that agreement had to be evaluated before the rate of return on the shares could be determined.

[1] February 1995, p. 196.
[2] T.M.A. 1970, s.42(4)(5), as substituted by F.A. 1994, Sched. 19, para. 13.
[3] Art. 24(3).
[4] SP2/95.
[5] *Finanzamt Köln-Altstadt v. Schumacker* [1995] STC 306.
[6] *Bachmann v. Belgian State* [1994] STC 979.
[7] A decision of the Special Commissioners: SC. 000020 (1995).
[8] I.C.T.A. 1988 s.709(2).
[9] [1993] STC 240.

CHAPTER 14

CLOSE COMPANIES

III. CLOSE COMPANIES: SECTION 419 LOANS

Disclosure

14–35

Note 19: *Earlspring Properties Ltd v. Guest* affirmed at [1995] S.T.C. 479.

CHAPTER 15

NON-RESIDENT COMPANIES, MIGRATION OF COMPANIES AND DUAL RESIDENT COMPANIES

II. COMPANY RESIDENCE

Treaty dual residence: the 1994 change

15–11   The Inland Revenue have published an article on the residence changes contained in Finance Act 1994 which contains a list, as at December 1994, of the United Kingdom's double taxation agreements showing those that do, and those that do not, contain a tie-breaker provision.[1]

Many tie-breaker provisions award residence to the country in which the place of effective management of the company is situated.[2] The Inland Revenue's view, set out in the Tax Bulletin article, is that in practice, effective management is normally found in the same place as central management and control, but this is not always the case.

Determining the location of the place of effective management requires one to have regard to all relevant factors (including the organisation of the company and the nature of its business) to establish where in substance the company is actually managed.

The new rule applies whether or not a claim for relief has actually been made under the double taxation agreement concerned. However, where the tie-breaker does not contain an objective test and so cannot be applied unilaterally but depends on agreement being reached between the two tax authorities concerned,[3] the new rules can only apply where a claim for relief has been made and residence has, under the tie-breaker, been determined to be located in the other country.

Footnote 5: Delete; see now, above.

IV. COLLECTION AND COMPUTATION OF TAX

Overview

The Finance Act 1995 introduces a new statutory code for the chargeability to tax of, and collection of tax from, non-residents and their United Kingdom representatives.[4]   **15–20A**

No liability is imposed on any United Kingdom resident person in relation to the non-resident's tax liability except where the United Kingdom resident constitutes a branch or agency through which the non-resident carries on a trade, profession or vocation—a U.K. representative.

The obligations and liabilities imposed on the non-resident are also imposed on the U.K. representative, subject to certain limitations where the U.K. representative is an independent agent.

Irregular agents, brokers and investment managers[5] even though constituting a branch or agency through which a trade is carried on are, subject to conditions, treated as not being U.K. representatives.

The above provisions replace those currently contained in sections 78 to 85 of the Taxes Management Act 1970.[6]

The United Kingdom tax liability of a non-resident receiving United Kingdom source investment income or trading income in respect of which there is, as a result of the broker or investment manager exemption, no U.K. representative will be limited to tax deducted at source. This statutory provision replaces Extra-Statutory Concessions B13 and B40.

U.K. representative—definition

Subject to certain exclusions (see para. 15–20D below), a branch or agency[7] in the United Kingdom through which a non-resident carries on (whether solely or in partnership) any trade, profession or vocation[8] shall be treated as the U.K. representative of the non-resident in relation to: **15–20B**

1. any income from the trade as arises, directly or indirectly, through or from that branch or agency[9];
2. any income from property or rights which are used by, or held by or for, that branch or agency[10];
3. any gains accruing on the disposal[11] of assets situated in the United Kingdom which are either used in or for the purposes of the trade at or before the time

23

when the gain accrued or which are used or held for the purposes of the branch or agency at or before that time, or assets acquired for use by or for the purposes of the branch or agency.[12]

The new rules bring the tax treatment of non-resident individuals broadly into line with that of non-resident companies.

Any liability or obligation imposed on a U.K. representative in relation to any income or gains continues, in relation to such income and gains, notwithstanding that the U.K. representative ceases to be a branch or agency of the non-resident.[13]

A U.K. representative that is a branch of the non-resident is treated as a separate entity from the non-resident and, where the U.K. representative is a partnership, the partnership "as such"[14] is treated as the U.K. representative[15]— the partners therefore become jointly liable.

Where the non-resident is a member of a partnership carrying on a trade or profession through a U.K. representative, the trade or profession carried on through the U.K. representative is taken to include the deemed trade or profession from which the non-resident's share in the partnership's profits or losses is treated[16] as deriving.[17] An "investor" in a trading partnership would, therefore, become subject to these rules. In such circumstances, if there is also a United Kingdom resident partner, the deemed trade of the non-resident partner is treated as being carried on in the United Kingdom through the partnership as such.[18] The partners therefore become jointly liable for tax on the non-resident partner's share of the United Kingdom profits.

U.K. representative—liabilities and obligations

15–20C The new legislation places the U.K. representative in the same shoes as the non-resident in connection with the assessment, collection and recovery of tax, or interest on tax, in relation to the trade carried on through the branch or agency: the obligations and liabilities of the non-resident are treated as those of the U.K. representative.[19] As a corollary, the discharge by either of any obligation or liability is also treated as a discharge of the corresponding obligation or liability by the other.[20] However, although the non-resident is bound by any acts or omissions of the U.K. representative, the reverse does not apply.[21] Where an obligation or liability only arises where some form of notice has been given, a U.K. representative must receive such notice in order to be subject to such obligation or liability.[22]

An independent agent[23] of the non-resident is not required, in relation to the provision of information,[24] to do anything which it is not practicable for him to do, acting to the best of his knowledge and belief and after having taken all reasonable steps to obtain the necessary information.[25]

Neither the U.K. representative nor the non-resident shall be guilty of a criminal offence unless the person concerned actually committed the offence or consented to, or connived in, its commission.[26]

An independent agent is given a statutory indemnity against the non-resident which includes the ability to withhold amounts out of sums due to the non-resident.[27]

U.K. representatives—exceptions

The following are specifically excluded from being U.K. representatives[28]:

1. agents not carrying on a regular agency for the non-resident[29];
2. brokers[30]; and
3. investment managers carrying out investment transactions for the non-resident.[31]

provided, in the case of 2 and 3, certain conditions are satisfied.

A broker will only not be treated as a U.K. representative in relation to transactions carried out for the non-resident if:

1. at the time of the transaction, he was carrying on the business of a broker[32];
2. the transaction was carried out by him on behalf[33] of the non-resident in the ordinary course of that business;
3. his remuneration is not less than that which would have been customary[34] for that class of business; and
4. the broker is not otherwise a U.K. representative of the non-resident for the chargeable period concerned.[35]

The protection accorded to an investment manager to prevent him being treated as a U.K. representative of the non-resident only applies in respect of investment transactions[36] undertaken for the non-resident. In addition, certain other conditions must be satisfied:

1. the investment manager must, when carrying out the transaction on behalf[37] of the non-resident, be acting in the ordinary course of a business of providing investment management services[38];
2. the investment manager must be acting in an "independent capacity" (see below)[39];
3. neither the investment manager nor persons connected with him must have a beneficial entitlement to 20 per cent or more of the income of the non-resident (see below)[40]—the 20 per cent test;
4. the investment manager's remuneration must not be less than that which would have been customary for that class of business[41];
5. the investment manager must not otherwise be a U.K. representative of the non-resident for the chargeable period concerned.[42]

In order for the investment manager to be acting in an independent capacity, the relationship between the investment manager and the non-resident must be such that, having regard to its legal, financial and commercial characteristics, it is a relationship between persons carrying on independent businesses that deal with each other at arm's length.[43] The Inland Revenue have provided non-statutory guidance, in the context of non-resident investment funds, as to the circumstances in which they would regard there to be such a relationship.[44] In general, the Inland Revenue would consider there to be such a relationship:

- where the provision of services to the non-resident (and connected[45] persons) is not a substantial[46] part of the investment management business;
- from the start of a new investment management business provided the above condition was satisfied within 18 months;
- where the investment manager intended to satisfy either of the above conditions and failed to do so for reasons outside his control, having taken reasonable steps to fulfil the intention;
- where investment management services are provided to a collective fund, the interests in which are quoted on a recognised stock exchange or otherwise freely marketed[47];
- where investment management services are provided to a widely held[48] collective fund.

Any case falling outside the above would have to be considered on its own facts.

As can be seen, in that context, the interpretation is sufficiently generous that only in very limited circumstances would the investment manager not be regarded as acting in an independent capacity.

In place of the connected persons restriction[49] which limited the application of the previous investment manager exemption, is the new provision that where the investment manager and persons connected with him[50] have a beneficial entitlement to 20 per cent or more of the taxable income of the non-resident, the whole of the income in respect of which there is such a beneficial entitlement can be taxed in the hands of the non-resident[51] and the investment manager is a U.K. representative in relation to such amounts.[52]

The investment manager is protected where there is a *qualifying period*[53] in relation to which it has been or is the intention of the investment manager (and persons connected[54] with him) that the aggregate of the non-resident's *relevant excluded income*[55] for that period should, as to at least 80 per cent, consist of amounts to which neither the manager (nor any connected person) has a *beneficial entitlement*.[56]

It does not matter that the intention is not fulfilled provided that such failure is due to matters outside the control of the investment manager (and connected persons) and the investment manager and such persons took reasonable steps to mitigate the impact of those matters.[57]

It is considered that *a beneficial entitlement to relevant excluded income* would not include the professional fees the investment manager charges to the non-resident provided such fees would be deductible[58] in computing the taxable income of the non-resident but would include carried interest in income or capital attributable to the manager or connected persons.[59] An investment manager could, therefore, be remunerated by a fee arrangement and take an interest of up to 20 per cent in the non-resident.

A reference to a *beneficial entitlement* of any person to relevant excluded income is a reference to so much of any amount (as is or would be attributable to that income) to which he has or may acquire a beneficial entitlement by virtue of any interest of his (whether or not an interest giving a right to an immediate payment of a share in the profits or gains)[60] in property in which the whole or any part of that income is represented or any interest of his in, or other rights in relation to, the non-resident.[61]

Concerns have been expressed in relation to the "old rules" that where the non-resident is a fiscally transparent entity such as particular types of offshore unit trust or partnerships, then as a result of the "see through" nature of the entity, the benefit of the investment manager exemption could be lost in the case of an investor in the non-resident fund where the investor is carrying on a trade and is connected with the fund's investment manager. The worry was that the non-resident's investment in the offshore fund could be regarded as an asset of its trade and therefore, to that extent, cause it to be regarded as trading in the United Kingdom. Where the non-resident was connected with the investment manager, the previous investment manager exemptions did not apply.[62]

The new rules deal specifically with the concern.[63] A fiscally transparent non-resident fund[64] is treated, for the purposes of the 20 per cent test only, as a company. If, as such, it would not be regarded as trading in the United Kingdom, the 20 per cent test is deemed to be satisfied.[65] If it would be so regarded, the "normal" rules apply although the fund continues to be regarded as a company.[66]

Non-residents: income tax limitation

Finance Act 1995 introduces a statutory code which replaces and extends the **15–20E** long-standing Inland Revenue Extra-Statutory Concessions, ESC B13 and ESC B40. ESC B13 (see paragraph 15–27 of the main work) limited the exposure to United Kingdom taxation of those entitled to take the benefit of it to tax deducted at source—the Inland Revenue would not seek directly to assess to income tax certain income received gross by the non-resident. ESC B40 limits the exposure to United Kingdom tax of non-residents trading in the United Kingdom through an investment manager who is protected from assessment by Section 78(2) of the Taxes Management Act 1970 or a broker who is similarly protected by Section 82(1) of that Act. Unlike ESC B13 and ESC B40, the new provisions contain no general tax avoidance caveat.

The new provisions apply with effect from 1996–97[67] except in relation to certain transactions carried out through brokers and investment managers, in which event they apply also for 1995–96 (see paragraph 15–20G below).

The income tax limitation is contained in Section 128 of the Finance Act 1995. The income tax chargeable for any year of assessment on the total income of any person who is not resident in the United Kingdom shall not exceed the sum of the following:

1. the amount of tax which would be chargeable on that total income less any *excluded income* and disregarding any personal reliefs; and

2. the amount of tax deducted at source from *excluded income*.[68]

For this purpose, *excluded income* is:

1. income in relation to which the non-resident does not have a U.K. representative (broadly, income not arising in respect of a trade carried on through a branch or agency (other than an irregular agent, a broker or an investment manager) in the United Kingdom); and
2. which is chargeable to tax under Schedule C, Case III of Schedule D, Schedule F[69] or trading income[70] in respect of which there is no U.K. representative because of either the broker or the investment manager exemptions.[71]

The effect of 2 above is that although an irregular agent through which the non-resident carries on a trade is not treated as a U.K. representative,[72] the liability of the non-resident itself remains.

The limitation on the United Kingdom tax liability does not apply to the income of non-resident trustees if there is a beneficiary of the trust who is either an individual ordinarily resident in the United Kingdom or a United Kingdom resident company.[73]

As mentioned above, the limitation on liability applies for 1995–96 and subsequent years of assessment but, for 1995–96 only, is confined in its application to transactions carried out through brokers and investment managers and, for this purpose only, the provisions of Sections 126 and 127 of the Finance Act 1995 are assumed to apply in relation to 1995–96.[74]

EXAMPLE

X Ltd. (a Channel Islands company) makes investments in the United Kingdom through a United Kingdom investment manager. X Ltd.'s income for the year 1995–96 comprises the following: net dividends of £80, interest of £75 (paid after deduction of tax of £25) and gross interest of £150.

	£
Total income	350
Excluded income	350
Tax deducted at source	45

X Ltd.'s United Kingdom tax liability is limited to the £45 regarded as deducted at source for these purposes.

Non-residents: corporation tax limitation

As one would expect, the corporation tax limitation is very similar, the **15–20F** corporation tax chargeable on the non-resident being limited to the aggregate of the following:

1. the amount of tax deducted at source from excluded income[75]; and
2. any corporation tax chargeable on the chargeable profits of the non-resident company if such profits did not include any excluded income.[76]

For these purposes, income is excluded income if it arises as a result of transactions carried out through a broker or investment manager who does not constitute a U.K. representative of the non-resident.[77] This provision therefore replaces ESC B40. A non-resident company trading in the United Kingdom is protected from assessment in respect of trading income arising through a broker or investment manager.

The limitation applies in relation to any accounting period ending after April 5, 1995.[78]

Timing

A broker or investment manager acting for a non-resident can rely on the **15–20G** existing rules for 1995–96 and the new rules for 1996–97 and subsequent periods.

Non-residents can rely on the new rules generally from 1996–97 and for 1995–96 in respect of transactions carried out through a broker or investment manager.

ESC B13 will, therefore, remain in existence until 1996–97 but because the new investment manager and broker protections apply, in relation to the non-resident, for 1995–96, ESC B40 was to have been withdrawn with effect from April 6, 1995. However, because of the concern that offshore fund structures set up before November 29, 1994 or being put in place in 1995–96 might not comply with the new investment manager provisions thus exposing the offshore fund to tax if ESC B40 were not available,[79] ESC B40 will continue to apply, where necessary, for 1995–96. Non-resident funds established in 1995–96 can therefore, for that period, take the benefit of either the new or the old rules. There is also an extra-statutory "grandfathering" concession which will allow funds set up before November 29, 1994 to take the benefit of ESC B40 beyond 1995–96.[80]

V. OTHER PROFITS CHARGEABLE

Gains of non-resident company imputed to shareholders: non-resident groups

Where it applies, the effect of section 13 of the Taxation of Chargeable Gains **15–28** Act 1992 is to treat the affected shareholder as if part of the chargeable gain had accrued to him. There is no actual or deemed disposal by the shareholder concerned. This may cause problems for tax exempt pension funds whose exemption from tax on chargeable gains only applies where the gain accrues to the pension fund from its disposal of an investment. Tax exempt pension funds may remain liable to tax where section 13 applies.

VI. STRUCTURING BUSINESS ACTIVITIES OF NON-RESIDENT COMPANIES IN THE UNITED KINGDOM: PRACTICAL CONSIDERATIONS

Distribution

Treaty Override

15–33 and 15–34

See paragraph 11–36A of this Supplement.

VII. INVESTMENT IN UNITED KINGDOM PROPERTY

Overview

15–39A

The Finance Act 1995 makes substantial changes to the income tax[81] rules which apply to the taxation of income from property. The motive behind the changes is simplification—to make it easier for those liable to income tax to compute their income from property and to assess it under the new self assessment regime. The changes took effect from April 6, 1995.[82]

The most significant change is in the basis of charge—henceforth, income from property will be regarded as a business, taxable under Schedule A (*a Schedule A business*[83]) and the majority of computational rules that apply to a Schedule D, Case I trade will apply to the profits or gains of a Schedule A business.

Interest relief will be available on a normal Case I basis, the existing restrictive conditions for interest relief being abolished. At the same time, the existing provision imposing a withholding tax on rental payments to non-residents will be repealed[84] and provision is made for regulations to be introduced governing the imposition of withholding tax.[85]

Schedule A Business

15–39B

Income tax is chargeable on the annual profits or gains[86] arising from any business carried on for the exploitation, as a source of rents or other receipts,[87] of any estate, interest or rights in or over any land in the United Kingdom.[88]

The reference to a business is extended to include isolated transactions,[89] thus bringing into charge one-off or casual lettings that would not normally be regarded as a business.

The existing exclusions from the Schedule A charge remain.[90]

Persons Chargeable

Persons receiving or entitled to the profits or gains of a Schedule A business will be subject to income tax under Schedule A on the amount of the profits or gains arising[91] in the year of assessment.[92]

The profits or gains (or losses) of a Schedule A business are to be computed as if that business was a trade, the profits or gains of which are chargeable to tax under Schedule D, Case I.[93] Where any person or partnership receives income from more than one property, the income from the properties will be pooled and treated as one Schedule A business. Property income arising in different capacities (for example, an individual owning properties and being a partner in a property owning partnership) will be treated as arising in respect of different businesses for the purposes of Schedule A.[94]

The change in the basis of charge under Schedule A for income tax purposes necessitates a number of consequential amendments to the Taxes Acts, including the Capital Allowances Act 1990.[95] The following is a brief list of the more important amendments—the reader is referred to Schedule 6 to the Finance Act 1995 for more detail.

It is made clear that a Schedule A business cannot come within Schedule D, Case I just because it would, on first principles, constitute a trade.[96]

The income tax charge on a Schedule A business applies, *inter alia*, to individuals and non-resident companies which are not trading through a United Kingdom branch or agency. The adoption of Schedule D, Case I principles for a Schedule A business would mean that interest paid to a non-resident would not be deductible in certain circumstances, for example, interest paid by a non-resident landlord to another non-resident would not be deductible.[97] This would impose a severe constraint on non-resident companies acquiring United Kingdom property and borrowing from a non-resident. This restriction on income tax interest relief is therefore disapplied in the case of a Schedule A business.[98]

Where there is a Schedule A loss[99] in any year of assessment, relief for the loss will be automatically carried forward and set against future Schedule A profits.[1] To the extent that capital allowances treated as Schedule A expenses exceed a balancing charge treated as Schedule A income, that part of the Schedule A loss may be set off against other (non Schedule A) income of the year concerned or the following year.[2] The carried forward Schedule A loss is reduced accordingly.[3] Unrelieved excess expenditure, losses and carried forward excess interest under the "old" Schedule A regime are treated as carried forward Schedule A losses under the new regime[4] provided the property continues to be let or, in the case of excess interest, provided interest relief would have been available for 1995–96 if the "old" regime had continued to apply.[5] The relief for pre-trading expenditure is extended, for income tax purposes, to a Schedule A business.[6]

Withholding tax

15–39D   Under existing law, there is a basic choice between arranging for rent to be paid direct to a non-resident in which case there is a withholding tax obligation[7] or making payment to a United Kingdom agent of the non-resident in which case there is no obligation to withhold but the United Kingdom agent becomes liable to income tax in the name of the non-resident.[8] Usually the agent would pay the money across to the non-resident but would receive an indemnity from the non-resident against any tax liability that might arise.

As a result of the general changes being made to the United Kingdom taxation liabilities of non-residents by Finance Act 1995, a branch or agency in the United Kingdom will as from 1996–97 only be assessable in the name of the non-resident where the non-resident is carrying on a trade in the United Kingdom.[9] See paragraphs 15–20A to 15–20G of this Supplement.

The provision effectively imposing a withholding obligation on direct rental payments to non-residents is being repealed in respect of payments made on or after April 6, 1996.[10]

In order to ensure that there is no loss to the Exchequer and to put in place a coherent regime, enabling powers are contained in Finance Act 1995 for the Board of Inland Revenue,[11] by regulations, to make provision for the charging, assessment, collection and recovery on or from specified persons of amounts in respect of Schedule A income of any person who has his usual place of abode outside[12] the United Kingdom.[13] Effectively, where the non-resident agrees to pay tax under the new self-assessment regime, rental income may be paid gross.

The following are specified persons:

1. a person by whom any sums are payable to the non-resident as fall, or would fall, to be treated as receipts of a Schedule A business carried on by the non-resident, for example, a tenant; or
2. a person who acts on behalf of the non-resident in connection with the management or administration of any such business, for example, a United Kingdom agent managing the property.[14]

Such persons have the benefit of a statutory indemnity from the non-resident and can retain amounts to satisfy liabilities out of any sums due to the non-resident.[15] The enabling powers are drafted very widely.[16]

Although regulations have yet to be published, it is understood that where the non-resident landlord chooses, by agreement with the Inland Revenue, to include tax on income from property in the payments on account made under self-assessment, the agent will have no responsibility to deduct tax at source. Subject to this exception, the specified person will have to deduct basic rate tax from property income, net of allowable expenses paid by the agent.

The specified person will have to account quarterly for the tax deducted and will have to provide the Inland Revenue with information regarding the income, the property or properties involved, the expenses paid by the agent and the tax deducted in relation to each non-resident landlord. It would appear that persons acting as property agents for non-resident landlords will be required to register with the Inland Revenue. Where income tax has been deducted, the specified person will have to provide the non-resident with a certificate detailing the tax deducted.

Relief for interest

Under the existing rules, relief for interest on a loan taken out to purchase property was only available (ignoring residential property) where the letting condition was satisfied—see paragraph 15–42 of the main work.[17] This, broadly, required the property to be let at a commercial rent for a period of time.

15–39E

Under the new Schedule A regime for income tax, interest expense will be available as a deduction in computing the profits or gains of a Schedule A business. The existing relief for commercially let property is, therefore, abolished as regards any payment of interest made on or after April 6, 1995.[18] There is a transitional provision for taxpayers whose Schedule A source income ceases in 1995–96.[19] Provision is made to ensure that interest expense is not relieved more than once.[20]

As the old relief was also relevant to corporation tax, it has effectively been retained for those purposes.[21]

Interest relief[22] is given effect to, for corporation tax purposes, as a charge on income.[23] Previously, relief for corporation tax purposes was given by reference to the income tax rules. This is not possible now that those rules have changed (for income tax purposes only) so the old code (see paragraph 15–42 of the main work) is re-enacted as a specific corporation tax relief.[24]

VIII. TRANSACTIONS REQUIRING TREASURY CONSENT

Movements of capital between residents of Member States of the European Union

Footnote 6—Austria, Finland and Sweden joined the European Union with effect from January 1, 1995—see paragraph 17–21 of this Supplement.

15–45

[1] Inland Revenue, Tax Bulletin, December 1994 at pp. 179 to 181. The list of the United Kingdom's double taxation agreements was updated in March 1995—see para. 17–01 of this Supplement.

[2] As is the case with the 1992 OECD Model Double Taxation Agreement.

[3] See the United Kingdom/Canada double taxation agreement.

[4] The new provisions apply, for the purposes of income tax and capital gains tax, in relation to the year 1996–97 and subsequent years of assessment and, for the purposes of corporation tax, in relation to accounting periods beginning after March 31, 1996: F.A. 1995, ss.126(9), 127(19), 128(7) to (11) and 129(5). Special rules apply, for 1995–96, in relation to non-residents whose United Kingdom branch or agent is a broker or investment manager: see paras. 15–20E and 15–20G.

[5] Certain protections also apply where the non-resident is a member of Lloyd's: *ibid.* s.126(1)(d).

[6] The "double foreigner" exemption (see para. 15–23 of the main work) is repealed and not replaced. Its repeal appears to leave open the possibility that tax liabilities could in future arise where, in the past, they would not have. For example, an investment manager who carries out transactions on behalf of a non-resident with other non-residents where such transactions are not "protected" investment transactions (see para. 15–20D below), such as commodity trading, will, under the new

rules, be assessable in the name of the non-resident whereas, in the past, T.M.A. 1970 s.82(2) would have provided protection. The Inland Revenue appears to take the view that *ibid.* s.82(2) is unnecessary on the basis that a non-resident trading in the United Kingdom is taxable only on the profits from the part of the trade carried on in the United Kingdom measured on the arm's length principle. On that basis, in the only cases which could fall within *ibid.* s.82(2), that would, according to the Inland Revenue, leave no profits to be taxed in the United Kingdom (after taking account of the arm's length fee payable to the agent). This approach was endorsed by the Financial Secretary to the Treasury when this point was raised during the Standing Committee debates: HC Official Reports, Standing Committee D, col. 547.

[7] As defined in T.M.A. 1970, s.118(1).

[8] For ease of reference, in the rest of this Part, the word "trade" only is used.

[9] F.A. 1995 s.126(2)(a). *Cf.* I.C.T.A. 1988, s.11(2)(a).

[10] F.A. 1995, s.126(2)(b). *Cf.* I.C.T.A. 1988, s.11(2)(a).

[11] The disposal must occur at a time when the branch or agency is continuing to trade in the United Kingdom: T.C.G.A. 1992, s.10(2).

[12] F.A. 1995, s.126(2)(c) which is actually worded by reference to T.C.G.A. 1992, s.10.

[13] F.A. 1995, s.126(3).

[14] Notwithstanding that, as a matter of English law, a partnership is not a separate entity from the partners.

[15] *Ibid.* s.126(4) and (5). *Ibid.* s.127(5) rather oddly refers to the branch or agency, rather than the trade, being "carried on".

[16] For the purposes of I.C.T.A. 1988, ss.111 or 114.

[17] F.A. 1995, s.126(6).

[18] *Ibid.* s.126(7).

[19] *Ibid.* Sched. 23, para. 1. *Ibid.* s.126(1) gives effect to *ibid.* Sched. 23.

[20] *Ibid.* para. 2(a).

[21] *Ibid.* para. 2(b).

[22] *Ibid.* para. 3.

[23] *Ibid.* para. 7. A U.K. representative will be regarded as the independent agent of the non-resident where the relationship between them (having regard to its legal, financial and commercial characteristics) is a relationship between persons carrying on independent businesses that deal with each other at arm's length. The absence of a shareholding relationship is therefore not determinative.

[24] "Information" includes anything contained in any return, self-assessment, account, statement or report that is required to be provided to, or to any officer of, the Board of Inland Revenue: *ibid.* para. 4(3).

[25] *Ibid.* para. 4(1). In such circumstances, the obligations of the non-resident itself are not discharged: *Ibid.* para. 4(2)(a). Also, the non-resident is not bound by any error or mistake made by the independent agent except where it arose as a result of his own act or omission or that of another to which he consented or in which he connived: *ibid.* para. 4(2)(b).

[26] *Ibid.* para. 5(1). A U.K. representative who is an independent agent shall not be subject to any civil penalty or surcharge provided it does not result from his own act or omission (or that of another to which he consented or in which he connived) and he can show that he would not be able to recover the penalty or surcharge from the non-resident: *ibid.* para. 5(2). It is not clear why this limitation is confined to independent agents.

[27] *Ibid.* para. 6. The indemnity is not limited to sums received by the independent agent on behalf of the non-resident and does not apply in favour of dependent agents.

[28] In each case in respect of income arising from, or other amounts chargeable by reference to, any business as relates to transactions carried out through the irregular agent, broker or investment manager concerned, including income from property or rights which, as a result of the transactions, are used by, or held by or for, that branch or agency: *ibid.* ss.127(1) and (15)(b).

[29] *Ibid.* s.127(1)(a).

[30] *Ibid.* s.127(1)(b).

[31] *Ibid.* s.127(1)(c). Certain persons connected with Lloyd's are also protected: *ibid.* s.127(1)(d).

[32] Where a person acts as a broker as part only of a business, that part is treated as if it were a separate business: *ibid.* s.127(14).

[33] For the purposes of *ibid.* s.127, a person shall be taken to carry out a transaction on behalf of another where he undertakes the transaction himself, whether on behalf of or to the account of that other, and also where he gives instructions for it to be so carried out by another: *ibid.* s.127(15)(a).

[34] Concern has been expressed that the use of the wording "customary" might exclude bespoke fee arrangements tailored to the requirements of particular clients, for example, volume discounts: HC

Official Reports, Standing Committee D, col. 546. The Financial Secretary to the Treasury did not comment on this point.

[35] *Ibid.* s.127(2). The broker could otherwise be a U.K. representative if, for example, he were also an investment manager as regards the non-resident but did not satisfy the conditions necessary to ensure that qua investment manager he was not a U.K. representative.

[36] "Investment transactions" means:
  (a) transactions in shares, stock, futures contracts, options contracts or securities of any other description, but not futures or options contracts relating to land; and
  (b) the buying or selling of any foreign currency or the placing of money at interest.
The Treasury may make regulations requiring other transactions to be regarded as investment transactions for this purpose. See *ibid.* s.127(12). The entitlement to settle a futures or options contract in cash does not prevent such contracts from being regarded as investment transactions: *ibid.* s.127(13). The existing wording in T.M.A. 1970, s.78(3)(b) covering transactions on a recognised futures exchange is not included, such transactions being covered by F.A. 1995, s.127(12)(a).

[37] For the purposes of *ibid.* s.127, a person shall be taken to carry out a transaction on behalf of another where he undertakes the transaction himself, whether on behalf of or to the account of that other, and also where he gives instructions for it to be so carried out by another: *ibid.* s.127(15)(a).

[38] *Ibid.* s.127(3)(a) and (b). Where a person acts as an investment manager as part only of a business, that part is treated as if it were a separate business: *ibid.* s.127(14).

[39] *Ibid.* s.127(3)(c).

[40] *Ibid.* s.127(3)(d) and (4).

[41] *Ibid.* s.127(3)(e).

[42] *Ibid.* s.127(3)(f). For example, the investment manager must not otherwise be the regular agent or "unprotected" broker of the non-resident.

[43] *Ibid.* s.127(18). This is the same as the "independent agent" test contained in *ibid.* Sched. 23, see para. 15–20C above.

[44] 1995 S.T.I. 283. The Inland Revenue have indicated that where the offshore fund is transparent for United Kingdom tax purposes (income is treated as that of the beneficiaries as it arises), the investment managment services should, for this purpose, be regarded as provided to the underlying investors in the fund.

[45] Where investment management services are provided to a collective investment scheme constituted as a partnership, participants in the scheme would not be regarded as connected persons for this purpose solely by reason of membership of the partnership.

[46] "Substantial" is regarded by the Inland Revenue as meaning "more than 70 per cent", either by reference to fees or to some other measures where that would be more appropriate. This test should be satisfied, in the case of a transparent fund, where it is the investment manager's only client provided that no underlying investor has an interest of more than 70 per cent in the fund.

[47] It is not clear what is required in order for a fund to be regarded as "freely marketed". Clearly the test will be satisfied where a fund is marketed to the public generally but the Inland Revenue have indicated that marketing to a more limited class of person would probably also be acceptable. This is important as the regulatory constraints on an offshore collective investment scheme are likely to prevent it from being capable of being generally marketed. In any event this has little practical application to fiscally transparent funds as the first condition specified above would normally be satisfied.

[48] This condition would be satisfied if either no majority interest in the fund was held by five or fewer persons and persons connected with them, or no interest of more than 20 per cent was held by a person and persons connected with him.

[49] T.M.A. 1970, s.78(5).

[50] Whether or not resident in the United Kingdom for tax purposes.

[51] The requirement of F.A. 1995, s.128(2)(b) is not satisfied.

[52] *Ibid.* s.127(8).

[53] The chargeable period concerned or a period of not more than five years comprising two or more complete chargeable periods: *ibid.* s.127(7). This is presumably intended to give protection against unanticipated events occurring within one chargeable period, for example, the redemption of shares or units by other investors in an open-ended offshore fund. A fund is open-ended if its shares or units can be freely redeemed at the option of the investor.

[54] Using the definition contained in I.C.T.A. 1988, s.839: F.A. 1995, s.127(17).

[55] The relevant excluded income of the non-resident is the aggregate of the profits and gains of the non-resident derived from transactions carried out through the investment manager and in respect of which the non-resident would not (assuming the requirement currently under consideration is satisfied) be subject to United Kingdom tax, other than tax deducted at source: *ibid.* s.127(5).

[56] *Ibid.* s.127(4)(a).

[57] *Ibid.* s.127(4)(b).

[58] It is understood that the Inland Revenue intend that the non-resident should be able to deduct items that would normally fall to be deductible in calculating a trading profit. The legislation is framed in general terms and not by reference to Schedule D, Case I principles in order to cater for non-resident funds that do not apply United Kingdom tax principles in computing their profits. Support for the Inland Revenue's approach can be found in *Fawcett v. Special Commissioners and Lancaster Farmer's Auction*: (1995) S.T.C. 61.

[59] 1995 S.T.I. 283 at p. 284. It is understood that, in the case of non-resident funds, the economical viability of the fund might be a factor to be taken into account, for example, if the fund would collapse without an injection of cash from the sponsor—usually the investment manager or a person connected with him.

[60] This is intended to cover both income profits and capital gains—I.C.T.A. 1988, s.833(1) is not regarded as applicable so as to exclude chargeable gains: HC Official Reports, Standing Committee D, cols. 546 and 547. F.A. 1995, s.125(5) refers to "profits and gains".

[61] F.A. 1995, s.127(6).

[62] T.M.A. 1970, s.78(5).

[63] F.A. 1995, s.127(9). The investment manager (or a connected person) can take an interest in up to 20 per cent of a transparent fund without automatically failing the 20 per cent test.

[64] In fact, the legislation refers to a "collective investment scheme" (as defined in the Financial Services Act 1986) which includes an open ended investment company which is not fiscally transparent for United Kingom tax purposes.

[65] *Ibid.* s.127(10).

[66] *Ibid.* s.127(11)—appropriate amendments being made.

[67] *Ibid.* s.128(7).

[68] *Ibid.* s.128(1). The reference to excluded income, the tax on which is deducted at source, is a reference to excluded income from which an amount in respect of income tax is or is treated as deducted, on which any such amount is treated as paid or in respect of which there is a tax credit and references to the amount of income tax deducted shall be construed accordingly: *ibid.* s.128(4). The reference therefore includes foreign income dividends (see Chapter 18 of the main work).

[69] *Ibid.* s.128(3)(a)—effectively replacing ESC B13.

[70] *Ibid.* s.128(3)(d)—effectively replacing ESC B40.

[71] *Ibid.* s.128(2) and (3). Certain other classes of income are excluded income including income chargeable to tax under Case VI of Schedule D by virtue of I.C.T.A. 1988, s.56 (again, covering ground previously protected by ESC B13) and certain welfare benefits (the latter having previously benefitted from an unpublished concession). The Treasury may, by regulations, designate other categories of income as excluded income for this purpose.

[72] *Ibid.* s.127(1)(a).

[73] *Ibid.* s.128(5) and (6). When the Finance Bill was first published there was a concern that this provision would prevent an offshore fund structured as a unit trust from being able to take the benefit of *ibid.* s.128(1) but the Inland Revenue have since confirmed that the provision is aimed at private trusts and is not intended to apply to commercial unit trust schemes. If the offshore unit trust is fiscally transparent so that the trust income is treated as the income of the beneficiaries as it arises, as will normally be the case, *ibid.* s.128(5) should admit of no application: there should be no question of the trustees of the unit trust being chargeable to United Kingdom tax at all—the Inland Revenue view I.C.T.A. 1988, s.59 as a collection mechanism rather than a charging provision.

[74] *Ibid.* ss.127(7) to (11).

[75] *Ibid.* s.129(1). The reference to excluded income, the tax on which is deducted at source, is a reference to excluded income from which an amount in respect of income tax is or is treated as deducted, on which any such amount is treated as paid or in respect of which there is a tax credit and references to the amount of income tax deducted shall be construed accordingly: *ibid.* s.129(3). The reference therefore includes foreign income dividends (see Chapter 18 of the main work).

[76] *Ibid.* s.129(1).

[77] *Ibid.* s.129(2).

[78] *Ibid.* s.129(5). The Guidance Notes issued at the same time as the Finance Bill refer, instead, to the limitation applying in respect of accounting periods beginning on or after March 31, 1996. As with the income tax limitation, the assumption is made, for accounting periods ending after April 5, 1995 but beginning before April 1, 1996, that *ibid.* ss.126 and 127 apply: *ibid.* s.129(6).

[79] The investment manager would still be able to rely on T.M.A. 1970, s.78(2) which applies until 1996–97.

[80] 1995 S.T.I. 283 at p. 285.

[81] The changes do not affect the corporation tax rules. The Financial Secretary has explained that the reason for this is that companies would otherwise lose flexibility: HC Official Report, Standing Committee D (Sixth Sitting), col. 166 (1995 S.T.I. 266).

[82] F.A. 1995, s.39(4)(a). The changes are disapplied for 1995–96 where the source of income affected ceases in that year: *ibid.* s.39(5). The Inland Revenue have also published transitional arrangements to deal with the change-over period: 1995 S.T.I. 250.

[83] A new definition is inserted in I.C.T.A. 1988, s.832(1) by F.A. 1995, Sched. 6, para. 28.

[84] With effect from April 6, 1996: *ibid.* s.40(3).

[85] *Ibid.* s.40.

[86] Which term does not include chargeable gains: I.C.T.A. 1988, s.833(1).

[87] The term "receipts" includes:
(a) any payment in respect of any licence to occupy or otherwise to use any land or in respect of the exercise of any other right over land; and
(b) rent charges, ground annuals and feu duties and any other annual payments reserved in respect of, or charged on or issuing out of, that land. *Ibid.* s.15(1)(3).

[88] *Ibid.* s.15(1), introduced for income tax purposes only by F.A. 1995, s.39(1). The "old" I.C.T.A. 1988, s.15 continues to apply for the purposes of corporation tax, creating scope for confusion.

[89] *Ibid.* s.15(1)(2).

[90] *Ibid.* s.15(2), replicating the "old" *ibid.* s.15(3).

[91] *Ibid.* s.21(2).

[92] *Ibid.* s.21(1) and (2), *ibid.* s.21 being inserted by F.A. 1995, s.39(2). The provisions of the "new" I.C.T.A. 1988, s.21 do not apply for the purposes of corporation tax: *ibid.* s.21(8). This replaces *ibid.* s.21(2).

[93] I.C.T.A. 1988, s.21(3). This is largely a helpful extension as, for example, the incidental costs of arranging loan finance will now be deductible: I.C.T.A. 1988, s.77. On a permanent discontinuance, Schedule D, Case I rules also apply: *ibid.* s.21(5). The new partnership rules introduced by F.A. 1994 apply immediately to a Schedule A business carried on in partnership. Various modifications to the Schedule D, Case I provisions as regards a Schedule A business are contained in F.A. 1995, Schedule 6: *ibid.* s.39(3). References in other enactments to Schedule A are to be construed as a reference to the new Schedule A regime: *ibid.*

[94] I.C.T.A. 1988, s.21(4). Profits and losses from all U.K. properties held in the same capacity will now be pooled, rather than each property being separately taxed, as before.

[95] Contained in F.A. 1995, Sched. 6. Capital allowances will generally be deductible as a business expense: *ibid.* Sched. 6, para. 8 and paras. 29 to 35.

[96] *Ibid.* Sched. 6, para. 2.

[97] I.C.T.A. 1988, s.82 which applies for the purposes of income tax only.

[98] F.A. 1995, Sched. 6, para. 13.

[99] Schedule A losses are to be computed in the same way as Schedule A profits, I.C.T.A. 1988, s.379A(7). The more generous Schedule D, Case I loss relief is not available.

[1] *Ibid.* s.379A(1), inserted by F.A. 1995, Sched. 6, para. 19(1).

[2] I.C.T.A. 1988, s.379A(2) to (10).

[3] *Ibid.* s.379A(3)(b).

[4] F.A. 1995, Sched. 6, paras. 19(2) and (3).

[5] Where there is carried forward interest on a let property it will therefore be important to maintain the commercial letting for 1995–96.

[6] I.C.T.A. 1988, s.401(B), inserted by F.A. 1995, Sched. 6, para. 20.

[7] I.C.T.A. 1988, s.43.

[8] T.M.A. 1970, s.78.

[9] F.A. 1995, s.126. T.M.A. 1970, s.78 is repealed with effect from 1996–97 or, for the purposes of corporation tax, in relation to accounting periods beginning after March 31, 1996: F.A. 1995, Sched. 29, Part VIII (16).

[10] *Ibid.* s.40(3). The obligation to deduct tax at source under I.C.T.A. s.119 is also removed in respect of rent paid after May 1, 1995: F.A. 1995, s.146.

[11] There was considerable debate in Standing Committee as to whether or not such wide powers should be exercised by the Treasury rather than the Inland Revenue: H.C. Official Reports, Standing Committee D (Sixth Sitting), cols. 170 to 174.

[12] The reference to "usual place of abode outside the United Kingdom" is no change from the present position: see para. 15–41 of the main work. The Financial Secretary to the Treasury has explained that the phrase means, simply, that the recipient lives outside the U.K.: H.C. Official Reports, Standing Committee D (Sixth Sitting), cols. 175 to 176.

[13] *Ibid.* s.42A(1), inserted by F.A. 1995, s.40(1). The regulations will apply to payments made on or

after April 6, 1996 and will apply both to income tax and corporation tax (in relation to the latter, in so far as the income would be included as a receipt in arriving at the income chargeable under Schedule A: I.C.T.A. 1988, s.42A(8)(a)). Where the income from the property is chargeable to corporation tax, *ibid.* s.42A applies to amounts chargeable under Schedule D, Case VI which would be chargeable under Schedule A if the non-resident were liable to income tax: *ibid.* s.42A(8)(b). No regulations have yet been made.

[14] *Ibid.* s.42A(2). There will be a final "settling up" with the Inland Revenue under self-assessment.
[15] *Ibid.* s.42A(3).
[16] *Ibid.* s.42A(4) and (6). Any interest required to be paid by any regulations shall be paid without deduction of tax and shall not be taken into account in computing any income, profits or losses for any tax purposes.
[17] *Ibid.* s.353(1)(b).
[18] F.A. 1995, s.42(1) and (3). A number of consequential amendments are required: *ibid.* s.42(2).
[19] *Ibid.* s.42(4).
[20] *Ibid.* s.42(5) and *ibid.* Sched. 6, paras. 17 and 18.
[21] I.C.T.A. 1988, s.338A, inserted by F.A. 1995, Sched. 7 for accounting periods ending after March 31, 1995: *ibid.* s.42(6).
[22] Available to a non-resident company under the code applicable to individuals: I.C.T.A. 1988, s.368(2).
[23] I.C.T.A. 1988, s.338(6)(d) and s.338A, both inserted by F.A. 1995, Sched. 7. The interests in land which can qualify for relief are restricted so as to exclude rent charges or the interest of a chargee or mortgagee: I.C.T.A. 1988, s.338A(10).
[24] I.C.T.A. 1988, s.338A, which effectively reproduces the "old" income tax rules in *ibid.* ss.353 to 368.

CHAPTER 16

CONTROLLED FOREIGN COMPANIES

I. OVERVIEW

16–01   Footnote 1—The Inland Revenue have issued[1] a new version of the Explanatory Notes for Controlled Foreign Companies. The revised version takes account of changes to the CFC legislation since 1990. The text and contents have also been amended in order to reflect the instructions which are given to Inspectors.

The internal Inland Revenue instructions on CFCs will be contained in the Corporation Tax Manual which is expected to be made available in late 1995. This will replace the Explanatory Notes which will not be re-issued or amended.

16–03   Footnote 17—Delete last sentence. See, however, paragraph 22 of SP1/90 and paragraph 15–11 of this Supplement.

16–04   The reference at the end of the second paragraph of this paragraph should be to sub-section 747(5)(b).

16–10A   When the acceptable distribution test for non-trading CFCs was changed from accounting profits to "net chargeable profits"[2] there was considerable disquiet as to the implications of having to treat the CFC as, effectively, a United Kingdom resident company in order to determine the level of acceptable distribution. In particular, concern was expressed as to the deductibility of interest payments made by the CFC[3] and the extent to which interest would be treated as a distribution.[4] The Inland Revenue have largely allayed these fears by means of an article in the Tax Bulletin[5] which seeks to explain how the Inland Revenue will deal with these (and other) matters in the context of the new acceptable distribution test and its practical application. When considering this particular aspect, reference should be made to this material as it contains a number of useful examples.

The Article foreshadows the informal clearance procedure subsequently announced (see paragraph 16–18A below).

As a result of a change made in Finance Act 1994[6] the acceptable distribution test for a non-trading CFC is 90 per cent of its "net chargeable profits' (see paragraph 16–10 of the main work).[7] This means that such companies will, in future, be required to calculate what their United Kingdom taxable profits would be in order to determine the appropriate level of distribution so as to meet the acceptable distribution test. In some cases this may be an onerous (and ultimately fruitless) task and, accordingly, it was considered at the time that there was likely to be a focus on other ways of avoiding an apportionment (see paragraph 16–10 of the main work). **16–18A**

In order to introduce an element of certainty and reduce companies' compliance costs, the Inland Revenue has announced[8] a new clearance procedure whereby it will be prepared to confirm, on the facts provided, whether a non-trading CFC meets the exempt activities or the motive test. Clearance is limited to non-trading CFCs in respect of accounting periods ending on or after November 30, 1993—the same accounting periods affected by the Finance Act 1994 change referred to above.

The Inland Revenue have indicated their willingness, in most cases, to give an advance ruling covering a number of years, provided all the relevant facts have been accurately disclosed and there is no change in the nature or conduct of the CFC's business.

CFCs generally operate and prepare their accounts in a currency other than sterling. When looking at their United Kingdom tax position, there is therefore the potential for a mismatch between economic profit and loss and tax profit and loss. Historically, this has not proved an insuperable difficulty as the only time a United Kingdom tax computation was relevant was when an apportionment was required. This necessitated the determination of "chargeable profits". **16–21A**

This issue has, however, been highlighted by two relevant developments. First, the new legislation for taxing foreign exchange gains and losses is now in force and requires a translation from foreign currency to sterling. Second, the acceptable distribution test for non-trading CFCs is now based on chargeable profits—the United Kingdom tax computation becomes relevant in determining whether or not a direction can be made.

The position for trading CFCs (affected only by the first development) was ameliorated by Finance Act 1994. Such CFCs which drew up their accounts in a foreign currency would have been required,[9] for the purposes of corporation tax, to compute their trading profits or losses in that foreign currency—see paragraph 16–21, footnote 16 of the main work.

The Inland Revenue denied a functional currency election for non-trading CFCs on the basis that a similar election was not available to non-trading companies in the United Kingdom whose profits and losses had to be computed in sterling. This ignored the obvious fact that, unlike most United Kingdom resident companies, a CFC is operating overseas in a foreign currency environment.

The Inland Revenue have now relented and new rules[10] require the chargeable profits of a CFC to be computed and expressed in the currency used in its accounts, whether it is a trading or non-trading CFC. As the change affects the calculation of chargeable profits it will impact on the acceptable distribution test for non-trading CFCs and the apportionment test for CFCs generally.

Notwithstanding this change, it is still possible for currency movements to give rise to tax charges, for example, a CFC based in the Netherlands which makes on-loans to United States companies in dollars, may find that when calculating its profits in guilders (which the new rules require) a change in the guilder/dollar exchange rate gives rise to a tax liability.

The new rules are linked to the application of the foreign exchange provisions and therefore references to a company's commencement day are to the first day of its first accounting period to begin on or after March 23, 1995.[11]

Where an apportionment direction has already been given under Section 747 of the Taxes Act 1988 as regards any accounting period of the company concerned beginning before the company's commencement date, the chargeable profits of the company for the accounting period starting on its commencement date and any subsequent accounting period[12] shall (notwithstanding any other rule, whether statutory or otherwise) be computed and expressed in the currency used in the accounts[13] of the company for the accounting period beginning on the commencement date.[14] It would appear that even if the company were subsequently to change the currency used in its accounts, the computation of chargeable profits would still have to take place by reference to the currency of account for the first accounting period of the company to which the new rules applied.

Where the company is a trading company but no such direction has been given, the new rule does not apply until there is an accounting period in respect of which a direction is given and the new rule will then apply for that accounting period and subsequent accounting periods.[15]

If no previous direction has been given and the company is not a trading company, the new rules apply for the first accounting period of the company as regards which either a direction is given or in respect of which it can reasonably be assumed[16] that a direction would have been given under Section 747 but for the fact that the company concerned pursued an acceptable distribution policy.[17] The need for the slight difference in treatment between a trading and non-trading company arises from the fact that in the case of non-trading companies, the chargeable profits calculation is relevant not only to the apportionment test but also to the acceptable distribution test. If the non-trading company would have been the subject of the direction but for it meeting the acceptable distribution test, the new rule will apply thus allowing the non-trading CFC perhaps to reduce the level of acceptable distribution required.

The chargeable profits of any company for any accounting period which begins on or after March 23, 1995 but before the new rule described above applies, shall (notwithstanding any other rule, whether statutory or otherwise) be computed and expressed in the currency used in the accounts of the company for the accounting period concerned.

The introduction of this new method of computing and expressing chargeable profits requires a number of connected amendments.

When considering the amount of the chargeable profits of the CFC to be apportioned to a company resident in the United Kingdom, the apportionment shall be calculated in the foreign currency and the apportioned amount shall be translated into sterling.[18]

Similarly, in determining whether a CFC direction is prevented because the £20,000 *de minimis* test applies, the chargeable profits of the CFC for the period shall be taken to be the sterling equivalent of its chargeable profits found in the currency other than sterling.[19]

When seeking to determine whether the CFC is subject to a lower level of taxation, its chargeable profits for any period should be translated into sterling.[20]

A number of consequential amendments are also made to Schedule 24 to the Taxes Act 1988 (assumptions for calculating chargeable profits) including one clarificatory amendment which appears to have no substantive effect.[21]

The capital allowances provisions of Schedule 24 of the Taxes Act 1988 are amended to take account of the fact that the CFCs chargeable profits will be computed and expressed in a currency other than sterling. Where a capital allowances computation requires account to be taken of earlier sterling amounts (for example, prior writing down allowances) such sterling amounts are to be translated into the appropriate foreign currency. In other cases, the necessary translation between sterling and the appropriate foreign currency (or vice versa) is to be made.[22]

[1] 1995 S.T.I. 555.

[2] F.A. 1994, s.134.

[3] Annual interest paid by a CFC, for non-trading purposes, to a person not resident in the United Kingdom would normally only be deductible as a charge on income if it was paid out of foreign source income: I.C.T.A. 1988, s.338(4). Short interest would generally not be deductible: *ibid.* s.338(3)(b).

[4] *Ibid.* s.209(2)(e)(iv) or (v), since repealed and replaced by s.209(2)(da).

[5] Inland Revenue, Tax Bulletin, August 1994, page 138.

[6] F.A. 1994, s.134.

[7] The change applies to accounting periods ending on or after November 30, 1993.

[8] 1994 S.T.I. 1343.

[9] The relevant provision (I.C.T.A. 1988, Sched. 24, para. 4A) has now been repealed and is deemed never to have been inserted: F.A. 1995, Sched. 25, para. 6(3).

[10] I.C.T.A. 1988, s.747A, inserted by F.A. 1995, Sched. 25, para. 2.

[11] *Ibid.* s.747A(9).

[12] I.C.T.A. 1988, s.747A(1), (5) and (6).

[13] References to the "accounts" of a company are to the accounts which the company is required by the law of its home State to keep or, if there is no such requirement, to the accounts of the company which most closely correspond to the individual accounts which companies formed and registered under the Companies Act 1985 are required to keep. For these purposes, the home State of a

company is the country or territory under whose law the company is incorporated or formed: *ibid.* s.747A(10).

[14] *Ibid.* s.747A(2).

[15] *Ibid.* s.747A(7).

[16] It is difficult to see how the reasonable assumption test will work in practice, given that any direction is at the discretion of the Board of the Inland Revenue. For example, a taxpayer could be left having to determine whether or not the Inland Revenue would apply the motive test in a particular case.

[17] *Ibid.* s.747A(8).

[18] *Ibid.* s.747(4A). The translation required is to be made by reference to the London closing exchange rate for the two currencies concerned for the last day of the accounting period concerned: *ibid.* s.747(4B).

[19] *Ibid.* s.748(4). The translation is to be made by reference to the London closing exchange rate for the two currencies concerned for the last day of the accounting period concerned: *ibid.* s.748(5).

[20] *Ibid.* s.750(6). The translation required is to be made by reference to the London closing exchange rate for the two currencies concerned for the last day of the accounting period concerned: *ibid.* s.750(8).

[21] F.A. 1995, Sched. 25, para. 6(1) and (2).

[22] I.C.T.A. 1988, Sched. 24, para. 11A.

CHAPTER 17

DOUBLE TAX RELIEF AND E.U. LAW

I. INTRODUCTION

17–01   Footnote 2—The Inland Revenue have published a revised United Kingdom treaty network as at March 9, 1995, together with a list of treaties under negotiation in Inland Revenue Tax Bulletin, April 1995 at pp. 212 to 214. See also [1994] S.T.I. 1362 for the Inland Revenue's negotiating priorities for double taxation conventions.

Unilateral relief

Chargeable gains

The Inland Revenue have published a new booklet[1] which lists all foreign taxes which the Inland Revenue have reviewed up to December 31, 1994 and shows whether they are considered to be admissible or inadmissible for unilateral relief. For completeness, the booklet also includes the taxes of countries that are covered by double taxation conventions. It should be stressed that the booklet only sets out the Inland Revenue's view and therefore, if the Inland Revenue do not consider that relief may be allowed for a particular tax, the taxpayer may appeal in the usual way. In addition, the Inland Revenue have stated that they will be willing to consider the admissibility of a foreign tax not listed in the booklet, or to reconsider a tax listed as inadmissible—if, for example, there is further information about it or the way it is applied.

It appears that the practice of the Inland Revenue is not to grant unilateral relief under Section 790 of the Taxes Act 1988 in respect of a foreign withholding tax which is only imposed where the recipient is a taxpayer in its jurisdiction of residence and is entitled to a foreign tax credit in that jurisdiction in respect of any such withholding tax.

III. MANNER OF GIVING RELIEF BY CREDIT

Whilst the company is free to allocate reliefs in as efficient a way as possible, it is important to note that the allocation of reliefs to foreign source income does not reduce the foreign tax credit attaching to such income.

EXAMPLE

X Ltd has a branch in Ruritania to which, in the year concerned, profits of £2,000 are attributable. The Ruritania tax rate is 25 per cent. The United Kingdom source profits of X Ltd are £500 and X Ltd has interest expense of £800 which qualifies as a charge on income.

	U.K.	Ruritanian Branch
Profits	500	2000
Charges on income	(500)	(300)
Taxable income	Nil	1700
U.K. tax		
at 33 per cent	Nil	561
Less foreign tax	Nil	(500)
U.K. tax payable	Nil	61

As the example shows, the charges on income can be allocated first to United Kingdom source income and then to foreign source income, so as to maximise the double taxation relief available. The double taxation relief available is not reduced to £425 (25 per cent of £1,700).

17–09   The European Commission has supported the Member States in their opposition to the imposition of unitary taxation.[2]

Following the United States Supreme Court's decision to uphold the right of California to impose its corporate franchise tax using a unitary method of taxation, the Inland Revenue has reviewed the basis on which tax credit relief may be allowed for the corporate franchise tax.[3]

Where a United Kingdom resident company has a branch which pays Californian franchise tax, unilateral credit relief will be allowed[4] for the lesser of:

1. the actual Californian tax paid, and
2. the amount of the tax that would have been paid on the basis of the profits of the branch which arise in the United States and the profits arising in the United States of any affiliated companies, to the extent that such affiliated companies are brought into the calculation of the tax as members of the unitary group or following a water's edge election.

The limit of credit for the Californian tax (plus any other taxes paid by the branch on its profits, including United States federal income tax) will be the United Kingdom tax on the profits of the branch which arise in the United States.

The same basis for quantifying the relief available is also to be used in the calculation of underlying tax where the Californian tax is paid by a company resident outside the United Kingdom which pays a dividend to a United Kingdom company and the companies are related to each other within the meaning of Section 801 of the Taxes Act 1988.

IV. E.U. Law

17–17   Footnote 15—The proposal for a Directive on a common system of withholding tax on interest income within the E.U. has now lapsed.[5]

Freedom of establishment

17–19   The provisions of the Treaty against discrimination embody common principles and accordingly decisions on one non-discrimination Article may be relevant in considering another. Accordingly, the personal tax case of *Finanzamt v. Schu-macker*[6] may have some application to corporate taxation, even though the relevant Article was Article 48 (free movement of workers). That case concerned a frontier worker, that is to say, one who lived in one member state (Belgium) and worked in another (Germany). Germany has progressive tax rates, and under domestic law allows income to be split between spouses where the taxpayer is resident in Germany or where he is resident in the Netherlands and derives at least 90 per cent of his income from Germany. The taxpayer in *Schumacker* complained that the refusal to allow him to split his income with his spouse on the grounds of his non-residence was contrary to Article 48. Nearly all his income was from his German employment, and in 1993 the Commission had adopted a recommendation that where at least 75 per cent of an individual's income is from the state where he works, he should not be subject to higher taxation in that state than would be payable if he resided there.[7] But this recommendation was not binding and the ECJ had to determine whether on the facts, Article 48 was infringed.

Germany, supported by other states submitted that personal circumstances should be taken into account only in the state of residence, because these were total income matters, and only that state claimed to tax total income. The general force of this submission was recognised, but it was held to be inapplicable to cases where the taxpayer's income in his state of residence was insufficient for personal reliefs to be given.[8] The principle here was that discrimination arises where different rules are applied to comparable situations or where the same rules are applied to different situations.[9] Here the taxpayer was in a comparable position to a resident of Germany and accordingly fell to be dealt with under the same rules. The Court also rejected arguments based on administrative and procedural difficulty.

So far as corporate taxation is concerned, the decision would be relevant to discriminatory rules governing the computation of total profits: it does not bear upon situations such as that considered in *Halliburton* where the tax charge was not based on profits, (but see the discussion at paragraph 12–31 of this Supplement). Of particular interest is the view taken of the "most favoured nation" treatment of Netherlands employees. The Advocate General in his Opinion used this circumstance to refute the German government's argument based on the cohesion of the tax system. He said:

> "... the German government cannot justify an infringement of art 48 by pleading the excessive financial consequences of making generally available a right which it has already granted to certain non-residents".[10]

This view appears to have been endorsed by the Court, but the passage is not as emphatic as that in the Opinion.[11] See paragraph 17–20A of this Supplement for further discussion of positive discrimination within the E.U.

–01 The United Kingdom subsidiary of the Germany company *Hoechst* has issued a writ against the Commissioners of Inland Revenue, seeking a declaration that the refusal of group income treatment to intra-group dividends is contrary to Articles 6, 52 and 58, and claiming compensation for breach of Treaty rights.

Footnote 20—The decision in *Bachmann v. Belgium State* can be found at [1994] S.T.C. 855.

Discrimination through double tax treaties

17–20A The subject of discrimination through bi-lateral tax treaties favouring one member state against others is discussed in great depth in an article in the E.C. Tax Review.[12] Of particular interest is the question of the extent to which member state A, by exempting residents of member state B from a provision otherwise discriminatory against all non-residents, may undermine a defence of that provision based upon coherence. It has been seen in paragraph 17–19 of this Supplement that in *Schumacker*, the Advocate General at least regarded the favoured treatment of Netherlands residents as incompatible with a coherence argument. In the U.K. one of the considerations that led to the revision of the thin capitalization legislation was the discrimination against residents of Ireland and Italy through the effect of the interest provisions in the treaties with all other member states.[13] Under the new rules, the domestic legislation is aligned with the OECD model article so that residents of countries without an OECD treaty with the United Kingdom are put in the same position as those of countries who do. The revisions do not entirely eliminate discrimination because under the treaty with Germany, ACT cannot be charged in respect of any interest treated as a distribution by virtue of I.C.T.A. 1988 section 209(2)(da).[14] Accordingly, to this extent, the position of the United Kingdom is "incoherent", but the implications are too uncertain to permit further comment. The Government, however, has no doubts:

> "As a further point, there has been some speculation about the possible relevance for the existing provisions of a recent European Court of Justice decision involving a Netherlands company (Halliburton Services BV). The Government intends the new provision [s.209(2)(da)] to remove any possible doubt this may have caused".[15]

VII. SUBSIDIARIES AND BRANCHES WITHIN THE EUROPEAN UNION

17–21 Pursuant to the Act of Accession 1994, Austria, Finland and Sweden joined the European Union with effect from January 1, 1995. The Council Directive of July 23, 1990 therefore became effective for all three new Member States as from January 1, 1995 and has consequently applied since that date to dividend payments made by or to companies in such Member States. The Directive contains a list of legal entities to which it applies in each of the 12 Member States which adopted it. The list of legal entities for the three new Member States can be found in the Appendices of the Act of Accession. There is no requirement for the Directive itself to be amended.[16]

It would appear that the Directive has now been incorporated in the laws of all Member States other than those member states who joined the E.U. with effect from January 1, 1995 (see above).[17]

Footnote 24—A reference has been made to the ECJ regarding the interpretation of Art. 3.2: *Denkavit International B.V. v. Bundesamt Fur Finanzen*.[18]

[1] I.R. 146 ("Double taxation relief—admissible and inadmissible taxes"): 1995 S.T.I. 518.
[2] 1994 S.T.I. 1653.
[3] Inland Revenue, Tax Bulletin, February 1995 at p. 194 and [1995] S.T.I. 304.
[4] Whether the tax is charged using the unitary method or on the basis of a water's edge election, *i.e.* on the basis of profits arising within the jurisdiction.
[5] 1994 S.T.I. 1386.
[6] [1995] STC 306.
[7] *Ibid.* p. 317d–e.
[8] *Ibid.* p. 326b.
[9] *Ibid.* p. 325a.
[10] *Ibid.* p. 319b.
[11] *Ibid.* p. 326e.
[12] The author is Luc Hinnekens: [1994] E.C.T.R. p. 146.
[13] [1994] S.T.I. 1495.
[14] See Article VII(1) which prohibits the charge to tax in the United Kingdom on interest payable to a German resident. However, Article VII(6) does not apply so as to allow the deduction of distribution interest in computing profits, because s.209(2)(da) is not limited to non-resident companies: see para. 11–36B of this Supplement and [1994] S.T.I. 1495.
[15] *Ibid.*
[16] See 1994 S.T.I. 1124.
[17] [1994] S.T.I. 1622.
[18] [1994] S.T.I. 1654.

CHAPTER 18

FOREIGN INCOME DIVIDENDS

II. PAYMENT OF FOREIGN INCOME DIVIDENDS

Taxation of recipient of FID

When a FID is paid to personal representatives, it is not treated as their income for income tax purposes.[1] Although, therefore, the grossed up amount of the FID will be treated as part of the aggregate income of the deceased's estate, it will not be taxed in the hands of the personal representatives. **18–04**

Theoretically, a non-resident company in receipt of a FID may be subject to a charge to income tax on the FID at the lower rate. The Inland Revenue have, however, stated that they do not intend to pursue any such liability.

The theoretical charge arises as follows. Income tax under Schedule F is charged on all dividends and other distributions made by a United Kingdom resident company unless they are specifically excluded from income tax.[2] Any Schedule F income of a person is charged to income tax at the lower rate, unless the person is an individual subject to higher rate tax.[3] This charge is not excluded in relation to a non resident company, whether or not it carries on a trade through a United Kingdom branch or agency, since distributions from United Kingdom resident companies do not form part of a non resident company's chargeable profits for corporation tax purposes.[4] Section 233(1) I.C.T.A. 1988 provides that no assessment to income tax at the lower rate is to be made on any person in respect of any distribution in respect of which that person is not entitled to a tax credit. This prevents a non resident company being assessed to lower rate income tax in respect of a normal dividend. While FIDs do not carry a tax credit, section 233(1) is specifically excluded where the distribution is a FID. As a result, there is nothing to oust the income tax charge at the lower rate. This was an unintended effect of the legislation and the Revenue have indicated that they will not take the point.

The significance of the point has in any event been diminished by section 128 of the Finance Act 1995.[5] This section broadly limits the theoretical income tax charge to the case where the non resident company has a United Kingdom representative in relation to the FID, that is, where the share on which the FID is paid is held by a United Kingdom branch or agency through which the non resident company trades.

III. COMPANIES OTHER THAN INTERNATIONAL HEADQUARTERS COMPANIES

Distributable foreign profits

18–09   A foreign source profit is an item of foreign income or a chargeable gain net of any deductions for expenses of management or charges on income which are allocated to it.[6] It follows from this that the calculation of foreign tax for the purpose of computing a distributable foreign profit differs from the calculation for the purpose of computing double tax relief.

The relevant amount of tax which is deducted from a foreign source profit in order to produce the distributable foreign profit may be different from the double tax relief which is available in respect of the income or gain represented by the foreign source profit because the relevant amount of tax is the foreign and United Kingdom tax payable on the income or gain, net of any deductions for expenses or charges which are allocated to it. Double tax relief, on the other hand, is calculated on the gross income or gain.

The point may perhaps best be illustrated by an example. Suppose that a company receives foreign interest of 100 from which foreign tax of 20 is withheld at source. Its net receipt is 80 and for both double tax relief and FID purposes charges on income of 30 are allocated to the interest receipt. Double tax relief will be the lower of the tax withheld (20) and corporation tax on the interest receipt net of the charges allocated to it ($70 \times 33\% = 23.1$). The corporation tax payable on the interest will therefore be 3.1 ($[(100 - 30) \times 33\%] - 20$). For FID purposes, the foreign tax payable in respect of the foreign source profit constituted by the interest will be 14 ($70 \times 20\%$).[7] It is clear that the amount of corporation tax payable in respect of the interest is 23.1 ($70 \times 33\%$) but is the amount of double tax relief for the purposes of section 246I(6)(b) 20 (the actual double tax relief in respect of the interest) or 14 (the tax withheld from so much of the interest as forms part of the foreign source profit)? It is thought that the latter is the correct sum, so that the amount of corporation tax in respect of the foreign source profit after double tax relief will be 9.1 (23.1 − 14). Consequently, the distributable foreign profit will be 46.9.

[1] I.C.T.A. 1988, s.246D(3A), introduced by F.A. 1995, s.76.
[2] I.C.T.A. 1988, s.20(1).
[3] I.C.T.A. 1988, s.207A(1).
[4] I.C.T.A. 1988, ss.6(2) and 11(2).
[5] See para. 15–20E of this Supplement.
[6] I.C.T.A. 1988, s.246I(1)(2)(3).
[7] I.C.T.A. 1988, s.246I(6)(a).

CHAPTER 19

PARTNERSHIPS AND EEIGS

Contents

II. COMPANY PARTNERSHIPS

Individual partners—"new" rules: simplified assessing

See, generally, Inland Revenue, Tax Bulletin April 1995[1] for an article **19–11** highlighting those parts of the self-assessment provisions which can have effect in 1994–95 and 1995–96 for income tax purposes, and indicating where relevant Inland Revenue guidance has been published.

As mentioned in the main work, Finance Act 1995 contains further provisions regarding the income tax treatment of partnerships. Section 111 of the Taxes Act 1988 is amended to clarify the rules introduced in Finance Act 1994 governing the computation of income and of basis periods for partnerships.[2]

As a result of self-assessment, changes are also made to the tax treatment of non-resident partners and non-resident partnerships.[3]

[1] At pp. 206 to 207. See also Tax Bulletin, December 1994 at p. 176.
[2] F.A. 1995, s.117.
[3] *Ibid.* s.125.

CHAPTER 20

INVESTMENT COMPANIES, INVESTMENT TRUSTS AND UNIT TRUSTS

I. INTRODUCTION

20–01   Footnote 1—On December 6, 1993, the Treasury published a consultative document containing proposals for a form of open-ended investment company (OEIC).

The intention was that OEICs should be taxed in a similar way to authorised unit trusts, with appropriate modifications.

The Finance Act 1995 contains an enabling provision[1] under which the Treasury may, by regulations, make appropriate provision in order to ensure that specified enactments shall have effect in relation to:

  (i) OEICs
 (ii) holdings in, and the assets of, OEICs, and
(iii) transactions involving OEICs

in a manner corresponding (subject to appropriate modifcation) to the manner in which they have effect in relation to unit trusts, to rights under, and the assets subject to, such trusts and to transactions for purposes connected with such trusts.[2]

The enactments specified are those relating to taxes on income, taxes on capital, stamp duty and stamp duty reserve tax.[3] For the purposes of taxes on income and capital, OEICs will be assimilated to authorised unit trusts. For stamp duty and stamp duty reserve tax they will be treated in a similar way to unit trust schemes as that legislation does not draw a distinction between authorised and unauthorised unit trusts. Any impediment to conversion of an authorised unit trust into an open-ended investment company will be removed.

The reason for such an enabling provision, rather than detailed legislation, is that at the time of Royal Assent to the Finance Act 1995[4] there was no corporate framework in existence for OEICs and therefore nothing on which detailed tax rules could be based.

In the Standing Committee debate on the provision,[5] the Minister of State, Treasury accepted that the situation was a little unusual in that general provision for tax treatment was being made even though no settled corporate framework was in existence but said that the Treasury would be publishing for consultation draft regulations providing for the corporate structure of OEICs.[6] Draft product regulations concerning the marketing of OEICs would be published, again for consultation, a few weeks later. The detailed tax rules, contained in regulations,[7] would follow once the non-tax aspects of OEICs had been finalised and would also be subject to consultation.

The lengthy tax and non-tax consultation process might delay the launch of OEIC's until January 1996, later than originally intended.

IA. VENTURE CAPITAL TRUSTS

The Government's proposals for a new tax advantaged investment vehicle have been enacted in Finance Act 1995.   **20–01A**

The new vehicle is called a "venture capital trust"[8] and is intended to encourage investment in small, unquoted trading companies.

Tax reliefs

In order to encourage individuals to invest in a venture capital trust, individuals aged 18 or over will be entitled to no less than four tax reliefs: **20–01B**

1. dividends (including capital dividends) paid by a venture capital trust will be exempt from tax but any associated tax credit will be recoverable[9]
2. gains on disposals of ordinary shares in a venture capital trust will be exempt from tax and losses will be non-allowable[10]
3. income tax relief at the lower rate (currently 20 per cent) is available on the subscription for new ordinary shares in a venture capital trust[11]
4. capital gains tax arising on the disposal of an asset after April 5, 1995 can be deferred where the gain is reinvested by such a subscription as is referred to in 3. above.[12]

The tax reliefs referred to in 1. and 2. above are limited to investments with a market value when acquired of up to £100,000 in any year of assessment—the company must be a venture capital trust when the shares are acquired. The relief described in 3. above is also limited to £100,000 of subscriptions in any year of assessment and, in addition, the shares must be held for at least five years and venture capital trust status must not be lost within that period otherwise there will be a claw-back of relief.[13] Where the £100,000 limit is exceeded, relief is still available in respect of the first £100,000 of investments. The Treasury have the power to make regulations in respect of such reliefs.[14]

The first three reliefs are subject to an anti-avoidance test.[15]

A detailed consideration of these reliefs is outside the scope of this work and the reader is referred to the legislation for more detail.

Venture capital trust: definition

20–01C Like an investment trust (see paragraph 20–12 of the main work), a venture capital trust is a company and is exempt from tax in respect of its capital gains.[16] Indeed, the venture capital trust regime is based very closely on the investment trust regime.

A venture capital trust is a non-close company which is for the time being approved by the Board of Inland Revenue.[17]

Approval[18] shall not be given unless it is shown to the satisfaction of the Board of Inland Revenue in relation to the most recent complete accounting period of the company that[19]:

1. its income in that period has been derived wholly or mainly[20] from shares or securities[21];
2. at least 70 per cent by value[22] of the company's investments has been represented throughout that period by shares of securities in *qualifying holdings*[23] of the company[24] (see below);
3. at least 30 per cent by value of the company's qualifying holdings has been represented throughout that period by holdings of *eligible shares*[25] (see below);
4. no holding in a company, other than a venture capital trust or a company which would qualify as a venture capital trust but for 5. below, has at any time during that period represented more than 15 per cent by value of the company's investments[26];
5. the shares making up the company's ordinary share capital[27] have throughout that period been quoted on the London Stock Exchange[28];
6. the company has not retained more than 15 per cent of the income it derived in that period from shares and securities.[29]

Where the Board of the Inland Revenue are satisfied that the above conditions are fulfilled in relation to the venture capital trust's most recent complete accounting period, the company shall not be approved unless the Board of the Inland Revenue are satisfied that the conditions will also be fulfilled in relation to the accounting period of the company which is current when the application for approval is made.[30]

Provisional approval may be granted even where the conditions referred to above are not fulfilled in respect of the most recent complete accounting period provided that the Board of the Inland Revenue are satisfied that any of conditions 1, 4, 5 and 6 will be fulfilled in relation to the accounting period of the company in which the application for approval is made (or in relation to the next accounting period)[31] or, in the case of conditions 2. and 3., that they will be fulfilled within 3 years.[32] In any such case, the Board must also be satisfied that the relevant condition will, once fulfilled, continue to be fulfilled in relation to subsequent accounting periods.[33] Approval can be withdrawn whenever it appears to the Board that there are reasonable grounds for believing that: approval was wrongly given[34]; a condition in respect of which provisional approval was given has not been, or will not be, fulfilled[35]; or a condition for approval has ceased to be fulfilled.[36] Subject to certain exceptions,[37] a withdrawal of approval shall have effect as from the time when notice is given to the company.[38]

It will be seen that the conditions are very similar to those applying to investment trusts[39] except that there is no requirement that:

1. a venture capital trust is resident in the United Kingdom for tax purposes;
2. the company's memorandum or articles of association prohibit the distribution as dividend of surpluses arising from the realisation of investments.[40]

It is not clear to what extent existing Inland Revenue practices (whether formal or informal) applicable to investment trusts will also apply, insofar as relevant, to venture capital trusts.[41]

Apart from the tax reliefs available to individual investors, a venture capital trust differs from an investment trust in three main respects.

First, in the case of an investment trust, approval is granted retrospectively for each period. For a venture capital trust, approval continues (once given) although, as mentioned above, it can be withdrawn in certain circumstances by the Board of Inland Revenue.

Second, 70 per cent by value of the venture capital trust's investments must comprise shares or securities in "qualifying holdings". For this purpose, "qualifying holdings" are, broadly, shares or securities of an unquoted[42] trading company, whether or not resident in the United Kingdom for tax purposes.[43] Investments in unquoted trading companies held by venture capital trusts at a time when such companies become quoted may be treated as investments in unquoted trading companies for up to a further five years.[44]

The shares or securities concerned must have been issued to the venture capital trust and at all times held by it.[45] The investee company must exist wholly for the purpose of carrying on one or more qualifying trades wholly or mainly in the United Kingdom and/or must hold shares or securities in, or make loans to, a subsidiary or subsidiaries[46] which so exist.[47] A trade[48] is a qualifying trade for these purposes if it neither wholly nor substantially consists of[49]

1. dealing in land, commodities, futures, shares, securities or other financial instruments;
2. dealing in goods (other than wholesale or retail distribution);
3. banking, insurance, money-lending, debt-factoring, hire-purchase financing or other financial activities;
4. leasing or receiving royalties or licence fees[50];
5. providing legal or accountancy services.

The money raised by the issue of the shares or securities must be used, or intended for use, for the purposes of the qualifying trade.[51]

The Treasury have power by order to amend, amongst other things, the definition of qualifying trade.[52]

Venture capital trusts may count investments up to £1 million in total in unquoted trading companies in any one year of assessment[53] towards the 70 per cent requirement,[54] provided that the gross assets of the company or group in which the investment is made do not exceed £10 million prior to the investment or £11 million immediately after it.[55] This latter limitation has caused concern in the venture capital/investment trust industry and is likely to limit the appeal of venture capital trusts to sponsors.

The winding-up of the investee company will not, of itself, cause the relevant requirements to cease to be satisfied provided such requirements would otherwise be complied with and the winding-up is commercial and not mainly for tax purposes.[56]

Third, 30 per cent by value of the venture capital trust's "qualifying holdings" has to comprise "eligible shares"—ordinary shares which carry no present or future preferential rights to dividends or to the company's assets on its winding up and no present or future preferential rights to be redeemed.[57]

II. INVESTMENT COMPANIES

Definition

20–02A The Special Commissioners have considered whether certain property management companies are investment companies.[58] The companies concerned collected income (such as service and maintenance charges) from residents and applied that income on the upkeep of the properties concerned. In each case it was determined that the business of the company concerned did not consist wholly or mainly in the making of investments but concerned the provision of maintenance services and, further, that the principal part of the company's income was not derived from the making of investments. The income derived from the obligation on the residents to pay an annual subscription to the company, it did not derive from the holding of land.

In the *Tintern Close* case, a number of principles were identified which could be applied in determining whether the business of a company consisted wholly or mainly in the making of investments:

(i) Was the company incorporated to acquire assets in order to turn them to account for the purposes of profit which could be distributed to shareholders?

(ii) What were the activities of the company?

(iii) If the activities of the company were concerned with the holding of investments, was the purpose of the investments to make money from them?

(iv) Did the purpose and nature of the operations of the company indicate that its main business was the making of investments?

In the third line of the second paragraph of this paragraph, "exepnses" should read "expenses".

Relief for losses on unquoted shares in trading companies

Losses arising to an investment company on the sale of unquoted shares in a qualifying trading company can, in certain circumstances, be treated as income rather than capital losses.[59] To be "unquoted", the shares must not be quoted on a recognised stock exchange.[60] A recognised stock exchange means the London Stock Exchange and any designated overseas exchange.[61] Shares dealt in on the Unlisted Securities Market are not "quoted" for this purpose.[62] The Financial Secretary has announced that shares dealt in on the Alternative Investment Market will also be regarded as unquoted for this purpose.[63] The Alternative Investment Market will replace the Unlisted Securities Market and the Stock Exchange Rule 4.2 dealing facility.

Interest

It is understood that there has been a decision of the Special Commissioners against the Inland Revenue's interpretation, holding that tax relief would be available when the bank debited the company's account in its books and not at any later time of actual payment.

IIA. CHANGE IN OWNERSHIP OF INVESTMENT COMPANIES

Introduction

It will be seen from paragraph 20–10 that investment companies are able to carry forward excess management expenses and excess charges on income. The amount so carried forward is treated in succeeding accounting periods (until exhaustion) as if it were an amount of management expenses incurred in those periods. In this way, the opportunity arises in each new accounting period to set off the excess expenses and charges carried forward against total profits. On this basis it has proved advantageous for groups to acquire companies with excess management expenses with a view to transferring to those companies new sources of investment income and assets with inherent gains.

Where there has been a change of ownership of an investment company,[64] the carry forward of excess expenses may be restricted in one of two ways. First, if in addition to the change of ownership there is a significant increase in the capital of the company or a material change in its business, then *all* further carry forward is prevented. Second, irrespective of changes in capital or in the business after the change of ownership, excess expenses cannot be carried forward and set against chargeable gains realised within three years on assets acquired after the change of ownership intra-group.

EXAMPLE 1

An investment company has excess management expenses in accounting period 1. In accounting period 2 it has a change of ownership and a material change in its business. In accounting period 3 it realises a chargeable gain on an asset it owned in accounting period 1. It cannot set off the excess expenses from accounting period 1 against the total profits of accounting period 3.

EXAMPLE 2

The same facts as above but without the change in the business. Here the company can use the excess expenses to reduce total profits in accounting period 3.

EXAMPLE 3

The same facts as in Example 2, but this time the asset is acquired intra-group in accounting period 3: the excess expenses cannot be used to reduce total profits insofar as those profits include the chargeable gain.

A further restriction concerns "excess overdue interest". This is interest which accrued before the change of ownership, but which is unpaid at the end of the accounting period in which the change occurs. It is, however, only "excess" if and to the extent that it exceeds certain profits of the accounting period in which the change of ownership occurs. Such interest is not deductible in computing profits. Without this restriction, excess overdue interest would become a charge on income for the first time when paid, and accordingly would escape the prohibitions on carry forward described above.

Thus, there are two sets of rules here. For these to apply there has to be a change in ownership, but then the general restriction on the carry forward of excess management expenses or excess overdue interest depends on there being also either a significant increase in capital or a material change to the business. Independently of whether there is any such increase or change to the business, there is a restriction on the use of excess expenses or overdue interest where gains arise on the disposal of assets acquired intra-group after the change of ownership.

These rules appear at first to be simply an extension of those familiar from other contexts which apply to past losses where there has been a major change in the nature or conduct of a trade, or which restrict the use of pre-entry CGT losses. However, the rules are in some respects of much more severe effect given the width of the meaning of "significant increase in capital", the possible total disallowance of excess management expenses even as respects income and gains from the pre-change part of the business (see Example 4 below) and the absence of any exemption for the acquisition of assets from pre-change of ownership associated companies.

General restriction on the use of excess management expenses

This restriction applies where there is a change of ownership and where one of **20–11B**
the following sets of circumstances exists:

(1) after the change there is a significant increase in the amount of the
    company's capital; or
(2) within the period of six years beginning three years before the change there
    is a major change in the nature or conduct of the business carried on by the
    company; or
(3) the change of ownership occurs at any time after the scale of the activities in
    the business carried on by the company has become small or negligible and
    before any considerable revival of the business.[65]

"Change in ownership" is governed by the rules[66] described in paragraphs 7–10
to 7–12.

Where any of the above circumstances apply, pre-change of ownership charges
and expenses cannot be deducted from total profits arising after the change.[67] The
restriction may be brought into play by events happening in accounting periods
following that in which the change of ownership takes place. For example, there
may be no significant increase in capital until two years after the change. In these
circumstances, the restriction still applies as from the time of the change, and an
assessment to recover any deduction allowed for an earlier accounting period may
be made within six years of the increase of capital.[68]

Of the three sets of circumstances, in practice it is the increase in capital
circumstance that is likely to be the most important. This is because it is easy to
increase the size of an already substantial investment business without altering the
nature of those activities (thus avoiding circumstances 2 and 3), but the definition
of substantial increase in capital is so wide that it is hard to do this without falling
into circumstance 1.

EXAMPLE 4

Take the case of a property investment company with two commercial
buildings. Each cost £1m. to build, but only one is let. The company is
capitalised at £2m. There are expenses of management brought forward of
£0.5m. being mainly interest referable to the unlet building. If the company is
acquired by a group and it buys another £1m. building with bank borrowing,
then the company will have significantly increased its capital. (It is clear that
neither circumstance 2 nor 3 applies).

For present purposes "major change" includes a change resulting from a
gradual process beginning before the six year period.[69] See paragraph 7–09 of
the main text for a discussion of "major change". "Significant increase in
capital" is considered in para. 20–11D below, but it may be mentioned here
that it is only increases within three years of the change of ownership that are
relevant.[70]

Where the restriction applies then the accounting period in which the change of ownership occurs is for present purposes divided into two periods at the point of change. There is then provision for apportioning expenses of management, charges on income and capital allowances of the true accounting period to the notional periods. This apportionment applies even to carried forward expenses because, of course, they are treated as arising afresh in each new accounting period. However, all excess management expenses brought forward from accounting periods ending before that in which the change of ownership occurs are apportioned to the first of the two notional periods and are disallowed accordingly.[71] As respects expenses, charges and allowances actually belonging to the accounting period in which the change occurs, expenses are apportioned according to when they are due for payment, interest is treated as accruing from day to day, and allowances are time-apportioned.[72] Balancing charges are not made for post-change periods unless there were sufficient profits to give effect to pre-change allowances.[73]

Excess overdue interest

20–11C   A payment of excess overdue interest is not deductible as a charge on income.[74] "Excess overdue interest" is a misleading term. It implies that interest comes within its scope only if it remains unpaid after the due date for payment. However, for this purpose, interest is deemed to become due on a day to day basis,[75] and accordingly, "overdue" means "accrued" but unpaid. This, of course, covers both interest that *is* overdue, and interest that has accrued on a day to day basis but which is not yet due for payment. In relation to a change of ownership, interest is overdue if it accrued before the change, and is unpaid at the end of the actual accounting period in which the change occurs.[76] Such interest is "excess" if and to the extent that it exceeds the amount of profits for the notional accounting period ending with the change of ownership.[77] "Profits" means profits after all reliefs and deductions.[78] For the rules governing the apportionment of profits see paragraph 2–20 of the main text.

Significant increase in capital

20–11D   As indicated above, it is significant increases in a company's capital that in practice are most likely to bring the restrictions into play. As will now be seen, this is because "capital" is widely defined to include certain debts. Thus, in addition to paid up share capital (including amounts in share premium account), and the amount of any redeemable loan capital, "capital" includes:

"the amount outstanding of any debts incurred by the company which are of a description mentioned in any of the paragraphs (a) to (c) of section 417(7)".[79]

The debts mentioned by s.417(7) are any debts incurred by the company:

(a) for any money borrowed or capital assets acquired by the company; or

(b) for any right to receive income created in favour of the company; or

(c) for consideration the value of which to the company was (at the time when the debt was incurred) substantially less than the amount of the debt (including any premium thereon).

Paragraph (a) of subsection (7) is clearly of general importance, covering as it does both the borrowing of money (for any purpose), and incurring a debt for the unpaid purchase price of a capital asset. Section 417(7) defines "loan creditor" and subsection (9) provides an exception from that category for banks lending in the ordinary course of business. However, this exception is not material for present purposes because we are concerned only with debts as described in section 417(7)(a)–(c) and not with the definition of "loan creditor". Accordingly, if an investment company borrows from a bank, it thereby increases it's capital.

Because the amount of a company's capital varies with the borrowing and repayment of loans, with the fluctuation of the sterling value of foreign currency loans, and the accrual of interest on loans, the rules determining whether capital has increased provide for a comparison to be made over time. However, the basic rule is that there is a significant increase in capital if capital increases by £1m. or doubles.[80] The amount of pre-change of ownership capital is whichever is the lower of the amount immediately before the change, and the "highest 60 day minimum amount for the pre-change year".[81] This is found by taking the daily amounts of the company's capital and determining the highest daily amount maintained for at least 60 days. The post-change amount of capital is the highest 60 day minimum amount for the three years after the change.[82]

Because pre-change of ownership debts are included in capital, a company does not increase its capital by turning such debts into equity.

Gains on assets acquired intra-group

The present rule applies where after the change of ownership, the investment **20–11E** company acquires an asset[83] intra-group and within three years of the change, the investment company realises a chargeable gain on the disposal of the asset.[84] In these circumstances, pre-change expenses[85] and excess overdue interest[86] cannot be set against an amount of total profits equal to the chargeable gain.[87] As mentioned, this rule does not depend on any changes to the investment business or to the capital of the company, and it is more severe than the pre-entry loss rules in that there is no exception for acquisitions from companies that were associated at the time of the change of ownership. Accordingly, if the A group is acquired by the B group, and after the acquisition, an investment company that was in the A group acquires an asset from another ex-A group company, the present restriction applies in the same way as if the asset had been acquired from a company that all material times had belonged only to the B group. The rule does not, however, apply where the disposal is more than three years after the change of ownership, even if the intra-group acquisition took place within those three years.[88]

III. INVESTMENT TRUSTS

20–12   A number of investment trusts invest in authorised unit trusts and, under a long-established practice, such investment trusts are able, provided certain conditions are met, to obtain approval. The existing Statement of Practice[89] has been revised[90] to take account of certain changes to the tax treatment of authorised unit trusts in Finance Act 1994.[91] The Statement provides that units in an authorised unit trust are regarded as shares in a company for the purposes of section 842 of the Taxes Act 1988. In addition, guidance is given as to the circumstances in which Condition 3 (see para. 20–12 of the main work) can be satisfied where an investment trust has a substantial part of its assets invested in an authorised unit trust.

Footnote 20—It is understood that the Inland Revenue take the view that, at least as regards investment trusts, short-dated debt (for example, certificates of deposit and commercial paper) do not constitute "securities" for the purposes of T.C.G.A. 1992, s.132(3)(b).

IV. UNIT TRUSTS

Authorised unit trusts: distributions

20–17   The Inland Revenue have confirmed that, when considering whether income is "eligible income" for the purposes of making interest distributions gross to non-residents, accrued income will follow the nature of the underlying income and an accrued income scheme charge under Case VI of Schedule D will be eligible income.

Footnote 8—To the extent that an interest distribution is sourced from eligible income (see para. 20–17 of the main work), payment can be made gross[92] by the authorised unit trust to persons not resident in the United Kingdom who make an appropriate declaration of non-residence.[93] Regulations have been made which modify the residence conditions and residence declaration where interest distributions are made to or received under a trust.[94] The Regulations also make provision enabling the Board of Inland Revenue to require authorised unit trusts to supply information and make records available for inspection in connection with residence declarations.

[1] F.A. 1995, s.152.
[2] *Ibid.* s.152(1).
[3] *Ibid.* s.152(2).
[4] May 1, 1995.
[5] H.C. Official Report, Standing Committee D (twenty-first sitting), cols 634, 636 and 1995 S.T.I. 474 and 475.
[6] Draft Regulations providing for the corporate structure for OEICs were made available for consultation at the beginning of May 1995: see Treasury Press Release dated May 2, 1995.
[7] Made under F.A. 1995, s.152.
[8] I.C.T.A. 1988, s.842AA, inserted by F.A. 1995, s.70.
[9] *Ibid.* s.332A and Sched. 15B, paras. 7 to 9. The Treasury are empowered to make regulations under

which the associated tax credit will be claimed by the venture capital trust and accounted for to individual investors: F.A. 1995, s.73(3). See The Venture Capital Trust Regulations: (S.I. 1995 No. 1979). The Regs. address: the procedure for approval of companies as venture capital trusts; the provision of certificates to investors to support claims for tax relief in respect of investments in venture capital trusts; and the procedures for securing tax relief in respect of distributions by the individuals beneficially entitled to shares in the company for whom relief is sought, before the venture capital trust can seek relief for such investors.

[10] T.C.G.A. 1992, s.151A. Where the approval of a venture capital trust is withdrawn, there is a market value deemed disposal immediately before venture capital trust status is lost (so that no taxable gain or allowable loss arises) and a reacquisition immediately after such status is lost.

[11] *Ibid.* s.332A and Sch. 15B, paras. 1 to 6.

[12] T.C.G.A. 1992, s.151A(3) and Sched. 5C. As the disposal of shares in a venture capital trust will normally be exempt from capital gains tax, the tax on the original disposal will become chargeable in certain circumstances, in particular when the shares in the venture capital trust are disposed of.

[13] Where the approval of a venture capital trust is withdrawn, there is a deemed disposal immediately before venture capital trust status is lost.

[14] F.A. 1995, s.73(1) and (2)(c). See the Venture Capital Trust Regulations: (S.I. 1995 No. 1979).

[15] This looks odd in the context of a vehicle which is designed to attract investment because of the tax reliefs available. When this point was raised in the Standing Committee debates, the Financial Secretary to the Treasury confessed that he had some sympathy with the point but said that the phrase was used in analogous situations and was used here "because it might otherwise be thought that a different regime was intended for [venture capital trusts]": H.C. Official Report, Standing Committee D (Eleventh Sitting), cols. 329 to 334.

[16] T.C.G.A. 1992, s.100(1) as amended by F.A. 1995, s.72(2).

[17] I.C.T.A. 1988, s.842AA(1). The Treasury have the power to make regulations in respect of the approval mechanism: F.A. 1995, s.73(2)(a). See the Venture Capital Trust Regulations: (S.I. 1995 No. 1979).

[18] Such approval shall have effect as from such time as may be specified in the approval, being a time which, if it falls before the time when the approval is given, is no earlier than:
   (a) in the case of an approval given in the year 1995–6, April 6, 1995; or
   (b) in any other case, the time when the application for approval was made.

[19] *Ibid.* s.842AA(2). There is a concern that the realisation of an investment and the receipt of cash proceeds could, by itself, cause one or more of the conditions (other than 5.) to cease to be satisfied.

[20] This will limit the ability of the venture capital trust to put cash awaiting investment on deposit.

[21] *Ibid.* s.842AA(2)(a). For the purposes of *ibid.* s.842AA, "securities" in relation to any company (whether the venture capital trust or any investee company):
   (a) includes any libility of the company in respect of a loan (whether or not secured) which has been made to the company on terms that do not allow any person to require the loan to be repaid, or any stock or security relating to that loan to be re-purchased or redeemed, within 5 years of the making of the loan or, as the case may be, the issue of the stock or security but
   (b) does not include any stock or security relating to a loan which has been made to the company on terms which allow any person to require the loan to be repaid, or the stock or security to be repurchased or redeemed, within that period: *ibid.* s.842AA(12).
It is not clear whether the right of a creditor to call for early repayment on the occurrence of an event of default will infringe the 5 year requirement.

[22] For the purposes of conditions 2, 3 and 4, this is taken to be the value when acquired unless the holding has been added to or a payment has been made: *ibid.* s.842AA(5). The requirement to revalue in such circumstances may cause difficulties if the venture capital trust is required to inject more capital into a company experiencing financial difficulties.

[23] *Ibid.* s.842AA(13) and Sched. 28B.

[24] *Ibid.* s.842AA(2)(b).

[25] *Ibid.* s.842AA(2)(c).

[26] *Ibid.* s.842AA(2)(d).

[27] Or, if there are such shares of more than one class, those of each class: *ibid.* s.842AA(2)(e).

[28] *Ibid.* s.842AA(2)(e). This is a slightly odd requirement given that a disposal within five years would prejudice the income tax relief available in respect of subscriptions by individuals.

[29] *Ibid.* s.842AA(2)(f)

[30] *Ibid.* s.842AA(3). There is no right of appeal—judicial review will be the only remedy.

[31] *Ibid.* s.842AA(4)(a). There is no right of appeal under *ibid.* s.842AA(4)—judicial review will be the only remedy.

[32] *Ibid.* s.842AA(4)(b).

[33] *Ibid.* s.842AA(4)(c).

[34] *Ibid.* s.842AA(6)(a).

[35] *Ibid.* s.842AA(6)(b).

[36] *Ibid.* s.842AA(6)(d). Where regulations prescribe further conditions in relation to the three year "grace" period for conditions 2. and 3., approval can be withdrawn where such conditions are not fulfilled: *ibid.* s.842AA(6)(c). Regulations may be made in respect of the failure to fulfil conditions and in respect of the withdrawal procedure: F.A. 1995, s.73(2)(d), (b) and (f). See the Venture Capital Trust Regulations: (S.I. 1995 No. 1979).

[37] *Ibid.* s.842AA(8) and (9).

[38] *Ibid.* s.842AA(7).

[39] Certain provisions of *ibid.* s.842 are borrowed and adapted by the venture capital trust regime: *ibid.* s.842AA(11).

[40] This may not be a practical possibility in any event, given the advance corporation tax liability that would arise.

[41] In a speech to the Association of Investment Trust Companies on May 16, 1995, the Financial Secretary to the Treasury indicated that where the venture capital trust legislation uses the same words as other pieces of legislation (such as the legislation governing investment trusts, Personal Equity Plans, the enterprise investment scheme and reinvestment relief) the Inland Revenue will use the same definitions and criteria.

[42] *Ibid.* Sched. 28B, para. 2.

[43] A detailed consideration of what constitutes a qualifying holding is outside the scope of this work and the reader is referred to *ibid.* Sched. 28B (inserted by F.A. 1995, s.70(2)) for the meaning of "qualifying holdings".

[44] *Ibid.* Sched. 28B, para. 2(6).

[45] *Ibid.* Sched. 28B, para. 1(2)(b).

[46] *Ibid.* Sched. 28B, para. 10.

[47] *Ibid.* Sched. 28B, para. 3.

[48] Which for this purpose includes research and development activities: *ibid.* Sched. 28B, para. 4(1)(b).

[49] *Ibid.* Sched. 28B, para. 4.

[50] There is an exception for research and development companies: *ibid.* Sched. 28B, para. 4(6).

[51] *Ibid.* Sched. 28B, para. 6.

[52] *Ibid.* Sched. 28B, para. 12. During the second reading of the Finance Bill, concern was expressed that the Government's objective would not be met and that low risk, property-backed venture capital trusts would be established merely as a tax-shelter. In response, the Financial Secretary to the Treasury said: "If there is evidence of the scheme being used for tax avoidance purposes or if a disproportionate amount of funds is invested in low risk activities, we shall not hestitate to take action to prevent this occurring. We shall make immediate use of the power in Schedule [28B] to add to the list of non-qualifying activities, if the need arises": H.C. Official Reports, Parliamentary Debates, Vol. 253, col. 422.

[53] Investments made within a six month period must be aggregated for this purpose: *ibid.* Sched. 28B, para. 7(5)(a).

[54] *Ibid.* Sched. 28B, para. 7. Where the unquoted company is carrying on the qualifying trade in partnership, or in a joint venture, with other companies, the £1 million limit must be divided by the number of companies involved.

[55] *Ibid.* Sched. 28B, para. 8.

[56] *Ibid.* Sched. 28B, para. 11.

[57] I.C.T.A. 1988, s.842AA(14).

[58] See *Tintern Close Residents Society Limited v. Winter*, and other similar appeals: 1995 S.T.I. 574 to 576.

[59] I.C.T.A. 1988, ss.573, 575 and 576.

[60] *Ibid.* s.576(4).

[61] *Ibid.* s.841. See para. 3–25 of this Supplement.

[62] Statement of Practice SP18/80.

[63] 1995 S.T.I. 343.

[64] As defined in I.C.T.A. 1988 s.130: *ibid.* s.768B(14).

[65] *Ibid.* s.768B(1).

[66] *Ibid.* s.769.

[67] *Ibid.* s.768B(9).

[68] *Ibid.* s.768(8) applied by s.768B(12).

[69] *Ibid.* s.768B(3).

[70] This follows from the definition of "the post change period" in Sched. 28A para. 4(2).

[71] I.C.T.A. 1988 s.768B(4)–(9), and Sched. 28A para. 7(1)(b).

[72] *Ibid.* Sched. 28A paras. 6 and 7. Where any of these methods would produce an unjust result, an alternative must be used: *ibid.* para. 8.

[73] *Ibid.* s.768(6)(7), applied by s.768B(12).

[74] *Ibid.* s.768B(10). A payment of interest on a debt is treated as discharging a liability to pay overdue interest in priority to other interest: Sched. 28A para. 10(2).

[75] *Ibid.* Sched. 28A para. 9(3)(a).

[76] *Ibid.* para. 9(2)(a).

[77] *Ibid.* paras. 11 and 12.

[78] *Ibid.* para. 9(3)(b).

[79] *Ibid.* para. 5. "Share premium account" is defined by reference to the Companies Act 1985, s.130. "Debt" includes accrued interest. "Capital" is expressed in sterling and rounded up to the nearest pound. There are no rules for determining exchange rates.

[80] *Ibid.* para. 2.

[81] *Ibid.* para. 3. The year referred to is the period of 12 months ending immediately before the change of ownership.

[82] *Ibid.* para. 4.

[83] Where the value of an asset is derived in whole or in part from the value of another asset, the two assets are treated as the same, so that if a lease is acquired intra group, and subsequently it is merged with the freehold reversion (not acquired intrao group), the disposal of the freehold within three years of the change of ownership would be subject to the present restrictions: *ibid.* s.768C(2).

[84] I.C.T.A. 1988 s.768C(1). Where the gain is realised in the accounting period in which the change occurs, it is treated as arising in a notional, post-change accounting period: *ibid.* Sched. 28A paras. 13(1)(a) and 15.

[85] Ascertained in accordance with the rules to the same effect as those described in para. 20–11B: *ibid.* s.768C(3)(4)(5), and Sched. 28A paras. 13, 16 and 17.

[86] *Ibid.* s.768C(9)(10).

[87] *Ibid.* s.768C(7)(8)(a). Where the gains of the period are reduced by losses, the restriction applies to net gains up to the amount of the gain on the asset in question: *ibid.* subs. (8)(b).

[88] *Ibid.* s.768C(1)(d).

[89] Statement of Practice SP5/91.

[90] Statement of Practice SP7/94 and see also 1995 S.T.I. 1152.

[91] See F.A. 1994, s.113 which provides that individual sub-funds of an authorised umbrella unit trust scheme are to be treated as single authorised unit trust schemes in their own right.

[92] I.C.T.A. 1988, ss.468M and 468N.

[93] *Ibid.* ss.4680 and 468P.

[94] (S.I. 1994 No. 2318); 1994 S.T.I. 1163 to 1166 and 1178.

PART II
GROUPS AND CONSORTIA

CHAPTER 21

GROUPS SUBSIDIARIES AND CONSORTIA: AN OVERVIEW

I. INTRODUCTION

The Finance Act 1995 has made two significant changes in relation to stamp **21–02** duty groups. First, the existence of a stamp duty group no longer depends on 90 per cent ownership of the issued share capital of the subsidiary but on 75 per cent ownership of the ordinary share capital.[1] Secondly, a new relief has been introduced for leases granted within a stamp duty group.[2]

[1] F.A. 1995, s.149, amending F.A. 1930, s.42(2).
[2] F.A. 1995, s.151.

CHAPTER 22

GROUP RELIEF

II. GROUP CLAIMS

Residence

The decision of the European Court in *Finanzamt Köln-Altstadt v. Schumacker*[1] **22–05** casts some doubt upon the ability of an E.U. company with a United Kingdom branch to surrender tax losses to or receive a surrender of tax losses from a United Kingdom resident group member, at least where the branch does not represent substantially the whole of the E.U. company's activities.

III. CONSORTIUM CLAIMS

Residence

22–19   See paragraph 22–05 for the implications of the decision in *Finanzamt Köln-Altstadt v. Schumacker.*

V. SECTION 410: ARRANGEMENTS

Consortium claims

22–58   In paragraph 22–58 of the main work, the authors drew attention to the potential problems that could arise where members of a consortium act together to exercise control over a joint venture company. Section 410(2)(b)(iii) of the Taxes Act precludes consortium relief where there are in existence arrangements by virtue of which:

> "any person ... either alone or together with connected persons, holds or could obtain, or controls or could control the exercise of not less than 75 per cent of the votes which may be cast on a poll taken at a general meeting of that trading company in that accounting period or in any subsequent accounting period..."

The connected person test is contained in section 839 of the Taxes Act.[2] Subsection (7) of that section provides that:

> "Any two or more persons acting together to secure or exercise control of a company shall be treated in relation to that company as connected with one another..."

When a joint venture company is formed, its shareholders will commonly enter into a shareholders agreement to regulate the joint venture. Will this mean that they are connected with one another and that section 410 therefore precludes consortium relief?

The question whether members of a joint venture who enter into a shareholders agreement are connected with one another arose in a different context in *Steele v. European Vinyls Corp (Holdings) BV.*[3] ICI and an Italian company, EniChem, had entered into a joint venture which held through the taxpayer company, a Dutch holding company, a number of subsidiaries, including a United Kingdom subsidiary. The question arose whether the Dutch holding company could claim a tax credit in respect of dividends paid by the United Kingdom subsidiary. Under the terms of the double tax treaty between the United Kingdom and the Netherlands this depended upon whether the Dutch holding company could show that it was not controlled by two or more connected persons any of whom would not have been entitled to a tax credit if he had been the beneficial owner of the dividends. EniChem would not have been entitled to a tax credit if it had received the dividends but were EniChem and ICI connected? The court held that this depended on the test of connection contained in section 839 and in particular on

68

section 839(7). The Dutch holding company was deadlocked at both board and general meeting level but ICI and EniChem had entered into a shareholders agreement. The court held that the shareholders' agreement constituted the necessary acting together to secure control so long as the parties treated it as in force.

There seems to be no reason in law why the decision should not be applicable to consortium relief. If, however, the decision were to be applied by the Inland Revenue in the context of consortium relief it would largely frustrate the purpose of the consortium relief provisions since there will generally be a shareholders' agreement between the parties. Prior to the decision the Inland Revenue had indicated to the authors that they would not treat members of a joint venture company as connected with each other for the purpose of section 410(2)(b)(iii) of the Taxes Act 1988 by reason only of their membership of the joint venture company. Given the practical implications for the consortium relief provisions, it would be surprising if *European Vinyls* were to lead to a change of practice.

IX. CLAIMS AND ADJUSTMENTS

Special arrangement

The special arrangement for group relief claims which applies to groups dealt **22–75** with mainly in one tax district may also be applied where it is convenient to do so and the companies are not dealt with mainly in one district. Further details of the special arrangement can be found in the Inland Revenue Corporation Tax Pay and File Manual.[4]

[1] [1995] STC 306, discussed at para. 17–19 of this Supplement.
[2] I.C.T.A. 1988, s.410(5).
[3] [1995] STC 31.
[4] Paras. 10603 *et seq.*

CHAPTER 23

CHARGEABLE GAINS AND GROUPS

II. INTRA-GROUP TRANSFERS

Exceptions

23–14   Before a company comes within the new regime for taxing foreign currency assets and liabilities, any foreign currency denominated debts on a security which it owns will be chargeable assets for the purposes of corporation tax on chargeable gains. After it comes within the new regime, they will be qualifying corporate bonds.[1] Similarly, foreign currency will cease to be a chargeable asset.[2] The new foreign currency regime applies for accounting periods beginning on or after March 23, 1995. If a group had companies with different accounting dates there would be scope for taking gains on foreign currency debts on a security and foreign currency outside the charge to tax. The company owning the debt or currency might, before it came within the new regime, transfer it intra-group to a company already within the regime. Section 171 would apply to the disposal and the gain on the debts or currency would therefore not be taxed. In order to prevent this, section 131 F.A. 1995 disapplies section 171[3] where a company disposes of a foreign currency asset before it comes within the new regime to a company which is already within that regime.

III. COMPANIES LEAVING GROUPS

Associated companies exception

23–26   The Finance Act 1995 has closed a scheme which exploited the associated companies exception to avoid a section 179 charge when a company left the group to which it belonged. The scheme worked as follows:

1. Suppose that a parent company, A Ltd, had a subsidiary, B Ltd, which owned an asset which it wished to sell for a price which would give rise to a chargeable gain.

2. B Ltd forms a new company, C Ltd, and subscribes shares equivalent to the market value of the asset. C Ltd uses the proceeds to purchase the asset from B Ltd.

3. B Ltd then issues sufficient shares to a third party to degroup B Ltd from the A Ltd group. No section 179 charge arises in respect of the asset owned by C Ltd because B Ltd and C Ltd leave the A Ltd group as associated companies.[4]

4. Finally, B Ltd sells C Ltd. No chargeable gain arises because B Ltd has a market value base cost for C Ltd. No section 179 charge arises because B Ltd was a member of the A Ltd group and not the B Ltd group when it transferred the asset.[5]

Section 49 of the Finance Act 1995 now prevents this scheme working by deeming B Ltd and C Ltd to have both been members of the B Ltd group when the asset was transferred between them. As a result, C Ltd would now suffer a section 179 charge in respect of the asset when B Ltd sells C Ltd.

Section 49 inserts three new subsections into section 179. These set out the circumstances in which the parties to the intra-group transfer are deemed to have been members of a different group at the time of the intra-group transfer. Where the associated companies exception has prevented a section 179 charge arising when a company left one group ("the first group") and the company subsequently leaves another group ("the second group") the associated companies will be deemed to have been members of the second group at the time of the intra-group transfer if there is a connection between the two groups.[6]

For this purpose, there is a connection between the two groups if the principal company of the second group is under the control of:

(a) the principal company of the first group or, if the first group no longer exists, the company which used to be its principal company;

(b) any company which controls the principal company of the first group or which has controlled it at any time since the chargeable company left the first group; and

(c) any company which has since the chargeable company left the first group controlled either a company which would have fallen within (b) if it had continued to exist or another company which would have fallen within (c).[7]

The connection rules are complicated by the need to prevent avoidance by putting new holding companies on top of the principal company of the first group and hiving up the controlling shareholding in the principal company of the second group or by allowing the controlling shareholding in the principal company of the second group to pass under the control of non resident associates.

It is important to appreciate that the new rules only apply where there is a connection between the group which the associated companies leave and the new group which they join. If there is no such connection, the new rules will not apply. Thus in Example 13 of the main work the result would be as stated in the text unless A Ltd controlled P Ltd.

IV. CAPITAL LOSS COMPANIES AND BOUGHT-IN ACT

Bought-in management expenses

23–39A   The Finance Act 1995 has introduced provisions to limit the use of surplus management expenses where there is a change in ownership of the company carrying them forward.[8] These provisions apply, in particular, where an investment company realises a chargeable gain on the disposal of an asset acquired after a change in ownership of the investment company from another member of its group. In such circumstances, the provisions may prevent expenses of management incurred before the change in ownership from being set off against the chargeable gain.[9] For further details, the reader is referred to the supplement to Chapter 20.

V. INTRA-GROUP SHARE AND DEBENTURE ISSUES

Intra-group share and debenture exchanges

23–41   The House of Lords have reversed the Court of Appeal's decision in *NAP Holdings v. Whittles*.[10] The case concerns the interaction of the rules for intra group transfers with the rules for share exchanges. Exco Overseas Ltd had acquired Astbro Inc for $7.5m. It transferred Astbro to one of its wholly owned subsidiaries, NAP Holdings U.K. Ltd, at a time when Astbro was worth $400m. NAP then sold Astbro and the question arose whether NAP's base cost was $7.5m or $400m. This depended upon whether section 171 T.C.G.A. 1992 applied or whether section 135 T.C.G.A. 1992 prevented section 171 applying with the result that NAP had a market value base cost. Section 171 applied:

> "where a member of a group of companies disposes of an asset to another member of the group."

Section 127 provided, however, that a share exchange:

> "shall not be treated as involving any disposal of the original shares or any acquisition of the new holding..."

NAP argued that because section 127 treated a share exchange as not involving any disposal section 171 could not apply. The House of Lords, upholding *Westcott v. Woolcombers Ltd*[11] held that this was wrong: section 127 only applied for the purposes of preventing the transferor company from realising a chargeable gain. It did not affect the transferee. Consequently, NAP's base cost was to be ascertained in accordance with section 171 and was $7.5m.

The decision in *NAP* is no longer applicable to intra-group share exchanges, since section 171(3) T.C.G.A. 1992 now provides that section 171:

> "shall not apply to a transaction treated by virtue of sections 127 and 135 as not involving a disposal by the company first mentioned in that subsection."

The decision remains relevant, however, where the share exchange took place before the enactment of what is now section 171(3) in 1988 and will, therefore, determine the transferee's base cost where the share exchange took place before then.

Doubt also exists about the position where the transferor in an intra-group share exchange has transferred shares for consideration consisting partly of an issue of shares and partly of cash. The basis for this doubt lies in section 171(3)'s reference to "a transaction treated by virtue of sections 127 and 135 as not involving a disposal". Where shares are exchanged for a combination of shares and cash, section 128 TCGA 1992 treats the transferor as having disposed of an interest in the original shares for the cash received. On a strict reading of the legislation, therefore, it would seem that section 171(3) does not apply and that therefore the taxpayer can still bring himself within the *NAP* decision by effecting the share exchange partly for cash. The main counter argument is based on the presumed policy intention behind section 171(3), the reversal of *Westcott v. Woolcombers*. It is very unlikely that Parliament intended to distinguish between shares exchanges where the consideration is entirely shares and share exchanges where some other element of consideration is also present. Whether the policy considerations could prevail against the strict wording of the sections is doubtful: the authors incline to the view that section 171(3) will not apply where the consideration for the share exchange is not exclusively the issue of shares and debentures. The Inland Revenue, however, take the contrary view.[11a]

NAP is also indirectly relevant to the determination of the transferee's base cost where there is an intra-group share exchange. It is considered that section 18 of the T.C.G.A. 1992 will deem the share exchange to be a transaction otherwise than by way of a bargain made at arm's length. Although section 18 only applies where there is both a disposal and an acquisiton *NAP* is authority for the proposition that from the transferee's point of view there is a disposal to him. Section 17 of the T.C.G.A. 1992 will then give the transferee a market value base cost. The limitation in section 17(2) will not apply because from the perspective of the transferee there is a corresponding disposal. The transferee will not, therefore, from a base cost point of view, need to be concerned about the value of the shares which it issues.

VII. OTHER MATTERS

Roll-over relief

Section 48 of the Finance Act 1995 has amended the rules relating to roll-over **23–55** relief within a group of companies in three respects. First, statutory effect has been given to the Financial Secretary to the Treasury's assurance that roll-over relief would continue to be available where one member of a group made a disposal and another group member made the acquisition of the new asset notwithstanding the decision in *Campbell Connelly & Co. Ltd v. Barnett*.[12] Secondly, the extra statutory concession for group property holding companies has been put on a statutory basis. Thirdly, the practice of obtaining unmerited roll-over relief by moving assets around the group has been curtailed.

It is provided that section 152 T.C.G.A. 1992 is to apply where the company making the disposal is at the time of the disposal a member of a group, the acquisition of the replacement asset is made by a company which is at the time of the acquisition a member of the same group and a joint claim is made as if both companies were the same person.[13] The existing law already provided that all the trades carried on by a group were to be treated as a single trade.[14] The joint effect of these rules is that roll-over relief is available where one trading member of a group disposes of an old asset and another trading member of the group acquires a new asset. The disposing company and the acquiring company need not both be members of the group at the same time. It is sufficient that they were members of the group in question when they made the qualifying disposal or acquisition.

Curiously, the provision treating the companies making the disposal and the acquisition as the same person only applies where a claim is made under section 152 of the T.C.G.A. 1992. No such provision is made for claims under section 153 where the consideration for the disposal of the old asset is only partially applied in acquiring a new asset. The Inland Revenue are understood to consider that the reference in the new provision to section 152 implies also a reference to section 153, and that the new provision would therefore apply to partial roll-over relief. This seems a surprising proposition when section 153 specifically states that section 152 does not apply in a case of partial roll-over and section 154 distinguishes between claims under section 152 and claims under section 153.

Where an asset which has been or is to be used only for the purposes of a trade carried on by the group is disposed of or acquired by a non trading group member, section 152 applies as if the non trading group member were carrying on the group trade.[15] Once again, although the new provision is stated only to apply for the purposes of section 152, the Inland Revenue are understood to consider that it applies also for the purposes of partial roll-over relief. Suppose that A Ltd owns a factory which it leases to another group member, B Ltd, which manufactures bicycles there. If A Ltd disposes of the factory and B Ltd applies the proceeds in acquiring replacement premises roll-over relief will be available on the making of a joint claim.

It used to be possible for a company which had realised a gain on the disposal of a qualifying asset to generate expenditure qualifying for roll-over relief by acquiring the trade of another group member. Suppose that C Ltd sold a factory used for the purposes of its trade for £1,000,000, realising a gain of £600,000. C Ltd could acquire the trade of another group member, D Ltd, and roll-over the gain into the expenditure it was deemed to incur in the acquisition of qualifying assets pertaining to the trade. D Ltd would not realise a chargeable gain because its disposal was intra-group and the group would not have to spend any money. This device was commonly known as "roll around" and was widely used. It is now provided that roll-over relief under section 152 of the T.C.G.A. 1992 is not available where a member of a group acquires the replacement asset on a no gain no loss disposal.[16] The device is, however, only partially blocked because the new rules do not apply to roll-over claims under section 153 of the T.C.G.A. 1992.

Although the Inland Revenue consider that the reference in the new rules to section 152 implies also a reference to section 153, this does not seem to be correct.

The rules treating group members as the same person and denying roll-over relief where a member of a group acquires an asset on a no gain no loss disposal are also applied to roll-over relief on the compulsory acquisition of land.[17]

[1] F.A. 1993, Sched. 17, para. 5.
[2] F.A. 1993, Sched. 17, para. 2.
[3] Along with ss.139, 140A, 172, 215, 216 and 217A T.C.G.A. 1992 and s.486(8) I.C.T.A. 1988.
[4] T.C.G.A. 1992, s.179(2).
[5] See para. 23–24 of the main work.
[6] T.C.G.A. 1992, s.179(2A).
[7] T.C.G.A. 1992, s.179(2B). The test of control is the section 416 test of control but a bank is not regarded as having control of a company by reason only of having or having exercised any rights in respect of loan capital or a debt for money lent by the bank in the ordinary course of its business: *ibid.* s.179(9A).
[8] F.A. 1995, s.135, Sched. 26.
[9] I.C.T.A. 1988, s.768C.
[10] [1994] STC 979.
[11] [1987] STC 600.
[11a] Inland Revenue Capital Gains Tax Manual, para. 45570.
[12] See para. 23–55 of the main work.
[13] T.C.G.A. 1992, s.175(2A).
[14] T.C.G.A. 1992, s.175(1).
[15] T.C.G.A. 1992, s.175(2B).
[16] T.C.G.A. 1992, s.175(2C).
[17] T.C.G.A. 1992, s.247(5A).

CHAPTER 26

RETURNS ON DEBTS BETWEEN ASSOCIATED COMPANIES

Contents   *Para.*

INTRODUCTION

In order to combat certain tax efficient structured finance transactions involving **26–01A** investment companies owned by banks, the provisions of sections 63 to 66 of the Finance Act 1993 have been adapted to apply also where a debt is owed to an associated company of a company carrying on a banking business in the United Kingdom.[1] As with sections 61 to 66, *simpliciter*, certain debts are exempted from the application of the new provisions.[2]

To achieve this adaptation, some amendments to sections 61 to 66 were necessary although no substantive changes were made.

Sections 63 to 66 have been rendered of general application by the substitution of "the creditor company" for "the resident company.[3] In addition, section 63(12) (definition of "commencement date") is repealed.[4]

Obviously, a connection between section 61 and the new "generic" provisions is needed[5] so a new section has been enacted.[6]

The new Section makes it clear[7] that where section 61 applies, references to the "creditor company" in sections 63 to 66 are references to the "resident company".[8] It is also made clear that the "commencement date" for the purposes of sections 63 to 66, as applied to section 61, is April 1, 1993.[9]

The above amendments are deemed always to have had effect and anything done under the provisions of sections 63 to 66 as originally enacted shall have effect as if done under, or by reference to, the provisions as amended.[10]

Qualifying indexed securities

26–13A   To address certain tax advantaged structures, qualifying index securities, the amount payable on redemption of which is determined by reference to the movement of a published index of prices of shares quoted in the official list of a recognised stock exchange, will not (in respect of disposals on or after November 29, 1994) be treated as qualifying corporate bonds.[11] This will be the case whatever the date of issue of the security concerned.

[1] F.A. 1995, s.89.
[2] *Ibid.* ss.89(2) and (3).
[3] *Ibid.* s.88(1).
[4] *Ibid.* s.88(3).
[5] *Ibid.* s.89 contains its own "connection" provisions: *ibid.* ss.89(8) and (9).
[6] F.A. 1993, s.62A, inserted by F.A. 1995, s.88(2).
[7] F.A. 1993, s.62A(a).
[8] Defined in F.A. 1993, s.61(1)(a).
[9] *Ibid.* s.62A(b).
[10] F.A. 1995, ss.88(4) and (5).
[11] F.A. 1995, s.50.

PART III
COMPANY RECONSTRUCTIONS

CHAPTER 30

CHANGE IN OWNERSHIP OF TRADE: CASE I IMPLICATIONS

VI. TRADING STOCK

Transactions between connected persons

The possible weakness of section 100 in relation to sales at an undervalue is **30–27** discussed in paragraph 30–36. Schemes to exploit the weakness involved the sale of stock within a group at below cost, with a view to deferring tax by the creation of a loss on the discontinuance. Such schemes are counter-acted by the amendment of section 100 as respects discontinuances after November 29, 1994.[1] As amended the section introduces new rules for sales and transfers between connected persons. For other sales and transfers the relevant figure remains either the money price or the value of non-monetary consideration.[2] Whether the sale is between connected persons or otherwise, it is specifically provided that the resultant figure is the opening figure for the purchaser.[3]

For connected persons,[4] the general rule is that the stock is treated as having been sold at its arm's length price,[5] but an election may be made by both parties for the greater of cost or the discontinuance price if the arms' length figure would be higher.[6] For this purpose, stock is taken in the aggregate. So, for example, if the cost of all the stock owned by A Ltd is 100, and on the discontinuance it is sold to a connected company for 100 but the arms' length price would be 120 both parties may elect for 100 as the discontinuance figure. If the price on the sale were 80, then by election, the discontinuance figure could not be less than cost (100). "Cost" here means the carrying figure in the accounts, normally the lower of cost or market value, but with a stock valuation immediately before the discontinuance.[7]

The connected persons rules do not apply to stock consisting of sovereign debt.[8]

---

[1] F.A. 1995 s.140(2).

[2] T.A. 1988 s.100(1A). Sales of animals within the herd basis are subject to special rules even if the parties are not connected: subs. (1B)(b) and Sched. 5 para. 5. Special rules apply to Building Societies on change of status: *ibid.*

[3] *Ibid.* subs. (1E). In s.100, "purchaser" includes any transferee: subs. (1G).

[4] "Connected persons" is defined by reference to *ibid.* s.839 with additional rules for persons controlling companies and for partnerships: *ibid.* s.100(F).

[5] *Ibid.* subs. (1A)(b).

[6] *Ibid.* subs. (1C). The election must be made within two years of the end of the accounting period in which the trade is discontinued.

[7] *Ibid.* subs. (1D).

[8] *Ibid.* subs. (1B)(a).

CHAPTER 31

STAMP DUTY

Contents   *Para.*

II. INTRA-GROUP TRANSFER RELIEF

Section 42: associated companies

31–12   The Finance Act 1995 has made two main amendments to section 42. First, the 90 per cent ownership requirement has been reduced to 75 per cent.[1] Second, a relief to the same effect as section 42 has been brought in for the grant of leases, agreements for leases and agreements for lettings.[2] Although the ownership requirement has been reduced, it is now measured in terms of "ordinary share capital", as against "issued share capital", so that fixed rate preference shares no longer count.[3] Direct or indirect ownership is established as before under rules[4] to the same effect as those set out in Chapter 21. So, for example, where A owns 80 per cent of the ordinary shares in B, and B owns 80 per cent of the ordinary shares in C, the 75 per cent relationship does not exist between A and C.

    The relief for the grant of leases is a new, self-contained provision, but it corresponds to the amended section 42 (as respects the tests of association)[5] and to section 27 (as respects arrangements).[6]

[1] F.A. 1930 s.42(2A)(2B), inserted by F.A. 1995 s.149.
[2] F.A. 1995 s.151(1)(6).
[3] F.A. 1930 s.42(2B), (4).
[4] F.A. 1938 Sched. 4 applied by F.A. 1930 s.42(3).
[5] F.A. 1995 s.151(7)–(10).
[6] *Ibid.* ss.151(2)(d)(3) and (4).

CHAPTER 33

BREAK-UP BIDS

II. BASIC TECHNIQUES

The main work discusses the possibility of using the demerger legislation to **33–02** effect the break-up of the target company after it has been taken over. It points out that the condition that the acquisition by third parties of control of any relevant company must not be a main purpose of any scheme or arrangements of which the demerger forms part is technically an obstacle to use of the demerger legislation in such circumstances. It is understood that it may no longer be possible to obtain Revenue clearance to use the demerger legislation as part of the arrangements for a break-up bid. It would be necessary to demonstrate that the demerger was not part of an overall scheme or arrangements encompassing the initial takeover.

CHAPTER 34

CROSS-BORDER MERGERS, DIVISIONS AND TRANSFERS OF ASSETS

Mergers and divisions

As noted in the main work, the United Kingdom has not implemented the **34–04** provisions of the Mergers Directive relating to mergers and divisions. The European Commission is currently assessing whether this is compatible with Community legislation.[1]

Transfers of assets

(b) Transfer of United Kingdom trade: capital allowances

34–10   The statement in paragraph 34–10 of the main work that where there is a transfer of part of a trade carried on in the United Kingdom the transferor's pool of qualifying expenditure is apportioned and no disposal value is brought into account is supported by the Inland Revenue's Capital Allowances Manual.[2]

(c) Transfer of United Kingdom trade: summary

34–12   Section 140 of the Finance Act 1995 has modified the position in relation to the transfer of trading stock.[3] Where A Ltd and B GmbH are not connected, the position is as stated in paragraph (iii) of the main text. Where, however, they are connected trading stock will be transferred at an arm's length price unless A Ltd, and B GmbH elect to transfer it at the higher of cost to A Ltd and the amount apportioned to trading stock on the transfer.[4]

(e) Transfer of non-United Kingdom trade: double tax relief

34–17   The Inland Revenue's Capital Allowances manual makes the point that there can be no credit for foreign tax "spared" under the Mergers Directive against corporation tax on balancing charges where there are no capital gains at all arising on the transfer of the non-United Kingdom trade.[5] This follows from the fact that the notional tax credit rules only apply where "section 140C of the Taxation of Chargeable Gains Act 1992 applies"[6] and that section only applies where "the aggregate of the chargeable gains accruing to company A on the transfer exceeds the aggregate of the allowable losses so accruing".[7] This limitation seems to be inconsistent with Article 10(2) of the Mergers Directive, which appears to require that the United Kingdom gives relief for the foreign tax which would but for the Directive have been charged on the profits giving rise to the balancing charge as if the foreign tax had actually been paid.

[1] [1994] S.T.I. 1622.
[2] Para. 571, which also explains the Inland Revenue's approach to apportionment.
[3] See para. 30–27 of this supplement.
[4] I.C.T.A. 1988, s.100(1A)(b) and (1C).
[5] Para. 595.
[6] I.C.T.A. 1988, s.815A(1).
[7] T.G.C.A. 1992, s.140C(1)(d).